Food to Love

Edward Hayden

THE O'BRIEN PRESS
DUBLIN

EDWARD HAYDEN works in Dunbrody Country House where he teaches in the Dunbrody Cookery School. Edward also teaches adult education courses in Waterford Institute of Technology and regularly lectures in Ryeland House Cookery School, Inish Beg Estate and An Grianan, ICA Adult Education Centre. Edward has a regular column in the *Sunday World*, has written for a number of local and national newspapers and has published recipes in the *Sunday Tribune*, *Irish Independent* and *RTE Guide*.

Edward's website, www.edwardentertains.com, has an up-to-date food blog and is packed with delicious and tasty recipes. His first book, *Edward Entertains*, is available from his website.

Dedication

I would like to dedicate this book to my father. Sadly, he passed away before it was taken on by the publisher and hit the 'big time'.
He always encouraged me to write this book and was constantly in my mind as I did.

Acknowledgements

Sometimes when we read a book we think only of the author and his or her workload. In truth, there are so many more people who must be considered. I was given tremendous support and assistance for this book, for which I am truly thankful.

First and most importantly I wish to thank my mum, Sally, who listened patiently as I tirelessly rattled on about this book. She always rowed in behind me in whatever way was required be it shopping for ingredients, peeling carrots or washing plates and was at all times the beating heart of the *Food to Love* engine.

My whole family gave me tremendous support and I would like to thank my sisters Anne, Esther & Lorraine, as well as my brother, Jim, for keeping me real and grounded throughout the process. Ironing shirts, making tea, washing pots and whipping cream are among the many and varied tasks they completed during the process! Special thanks also to my niece, Marie, who joined Mum and I for some of the photographs – she always smiled on request!

My good friend, colleague and confidant Lorain Walsh again pitched in and read all of the recipes for me to ensure culinary accuracy and coherence. Her attention to detail and willingness to critique this book has helped to shape it and it is something I very much appreciate.

They say when you work you should surround yourself with talented people and in terms of my chosen photographer that is indeed what I did. Carol Marks of Carol Marks Photography worked with me on my first cookery book, *Edward Entertains*, and her work on that book was complimented and commended so often that it was to my delight that she made herself available again to work on this book. Photography is such an important element of any cookery book and yet again Carol has delivered photography that surpassed all of my expectations.

I would like to pay special tribute to the team at The O'Brien Press. To Michael O'Brien, Mary Webb, Helen Carr, Emma Byrne, Donna Sørenson, Gráinne Killeen and all the team I would like to express a heartfelt thanks. They have taken me every step of the way. Their willingness for discourse, their genuine interest in my input and their ability to turn my typed files into a work of art have made this a journey both magical and exciting.

Finally to all my extended family and friends to whom I have chatted about this book for the last twelve months ... thanks for listening!

First published 2011 by The O'Brien Press Ltd,
12 Terenure Road East, Rathgar, Dublin 6, Ireland.
Tel: +353 1 4923333; Fax: +353 1 4922777
E-mail: books@obrien.ie
Website: www.obrien.ie

ISBN: 978-1-84717-246-4

A catalogue record of this title is available from The British Library

1 2 3 4 5 6 7 8 9 10
11 12 13 14 15 16 17

Printed and bound in Italy by Rotolito Lombarda S.p.A.
The paper used in this book is produced using pulp from managed forests.

contents

introduction

As you go through life, certain days stand out more than others. On my twenty-seventh birthday, 10 June 2010, I got a phone call from Michael O'Brien to say that The O'Brien Press were going to publish my cookery book. What a day and what a birthday present! A phone call like this says many things, but above all it says, 'We believe in you'. And so begins the story of Edward Hayden, *Food to Love* and The O'Brien Press.

We came up with the title, *Food to Love,* because I really wanted the book to be representative of the food that I love to serve and eat. When I give people a recipe, my favourite response is, 'Oh Edward, I tried out that recipe and it worked really well!', so with this in mind I planned the recipes very carefully from a number of different perspectives. I like to supply recipes that are not overly labour-intensive, for which the ingredients can be sourced readily and that

will work out. I've tried to include recipes for all culinary occasions.

I always say that food is one of the greatest topics of conversation and no gathering of people, either food-related or not, ends without a full discussion on food, chefs, restaurants or recipes. It's a universal vernacular and it seems that food, in some guise or other, is of interest to everyone.

Food styles and trends are changing so much these days that it is hard to keep up, but 'home cooking', is a recurring style and trend, because there's something very satisfying about spending time cooking and serving a delicious home-cooked meal to family and friends. I hope that this book will show you that you can entertain at home with the greatest of ease and create lasting gastronomic memories with a little help from *Food to Love*.

Happy Cooking!

Edward

light bites

Leabharlanna Fhine Gall

Creamy Leek & Smoked Salmon Tart _Serves 8-10_

This is a favourite of mine and it can be served as either a substantial starter or a light main course. The pastry for this dish can made and frozen in advance; you could even make double so that you'd have a supply in the freezer! Try experimenting using other varieties of fillings in this dish instead of the smoked salmon, such as smoked bacon or chorizo.

Shortcrust Pastry:
7oz/200g plain flour
3½ oz/100g hard butter
Pinch of salt
Ice cold water (6-8 dessertspoons, approx)

Filling:
2 small leeks
1oz/25g butter
3 large free range eggs
9floz/250ml milk
2floz/50ml pouring cream
6oz/175g smoked salmon
Salt & freshly-ground black pepper
4oz/110g grated cheddar cheese

Begin by making the pastry. Sieve the plain flour into a large mixing bowl. Add in the pinch of salt. Cut the butter into pieces and add this to the flour and salt. Using the tips of your fingers rub the butter into the flour until the mixture resembles fine breadcrumbs.

Next mix in the water, gradually, until the mixture all comes together into a ball. Knead lightly to achieve a smooth pastry and then wrap it in cling film and refrigerate for at least an hour, but for longer if time will allow.

Preheat the oven to 180C/350F/Gas Mark 4.

Roll out the pastry and use it to line a 10inch/25cm loose-bottomed flan ring or a large ceramic quiche dish. Blind bake the pastry (see opposite) and allow to cool down.

Meanwhile wash and thinly slice the leeks.

Heat the butter in a medium-sized frying pan, add the leeks and cook on a gentle heat until they have softened down. This will probably take about ten minutes on a low heat.

Season with black pepper and transfer to a bowl and allow the mixture to cool down.

Whilst waiting for the leeks to cool down, take a large mixing bowl and whisk the eggs, milk and cream together to form an egg custard.

When the leeks have cooled sufficiently spread them over the base of the blind-baked pastry. Cut the smoked salmon into cubes and place this on top of the leeks.

Pour the whisked egg custard on top of the leek mixture and sprinkle with the grated cheese. Transfer the entire dish to the preheated oven.

Bake for 30-35 minutes or until the pastry is cooked through and the egg custard has set sufficiently around the leeks. There may still be a little wobble in the centre, but that's fine.

Remove from the oven and allow the tart to rest for at least 10-12 minutes before cutting and serving.

Serve with a large salad.

How To Bake Blind:

Line your chosen tin with your chosen pastry.

Next cover the pastry-lined tartlet mould with a triple layer of cling film, fill with rice/lentils/chickpeas and cover over with another layer of cling film.

Place this in the oven (180C/350F/Gas Mark 4) for 15 minutes and then remove the rice parcel and bake the pastry for a further eight minutes.

This leaves you with a perfect tartlet shell whose sides will not fall in.

If you wish, having removed the rice parcel, you could brush the pastry with a little egg white before re-baking to harden up the pastry and prevent it from becoming soggy later on.

Make sure to use plenty of cling film and overlap it to prevent it from melting in the oven. Retain the dry ingredients for future blind baking as they are now, no longer suitable for cooking.

You can use a layer of parchment paper instead of the cling film.

Homemade Caesar Salad with Oven-Poached Chicken Serves 6

So many of us like Caesar salad when we go out to eat, but it's also quite simple to prepare at home. There are just four basic steps: poaching the chicken, preparing the croutons, making the dressing and putting the salad together. I love this method of poaching the chicken as it keeps the chicken really moist and very easy to slice. By using convenience mayonnaise I have made a 'cheat's version' of the classic Caesar dressing which uses raw egg yolks as the base for the dressing

Caesar Salad:

2 small heads cos lettuce
Crispy garlic croutons (see below)
6oz/175g bacon lardons
Caesar Dressing (see below right)
4 breasts oven-poached chicken (see right)
4oz/110g grated parmesan

Heat a small pan and dry fry the bacon lardons until crisp. Drain onto kitchen paper and store until required.

Crispy Garlic Croutons:

2 cloves of garlic, finely chopped
1 dessertspoon of parsley, chopped
6 thick-cut slices of bread
1oz/25g butter
Salt & freshly-ground pepper

Preheat the oven to 190C/325F/Gas Mark 5.
Mix the garlic, parsley and butter together.
Spread the garlic and herb butter onto the sliced bread and then remove the crusts and cut into small dice.
Place the diced bread onto a flat baking tray and bake the for 10-12 minutes in the preheated oven.
Drain on kitchen paper and retain until you are assembling the salad.

Oven-Poached Chicken:

4 chicken breasts
Cracked black pepper
2-3 parsley stalks
6floz/150ml/1 glass of white wine
6floz/150ml/1 glass of water

Preheat oven to 170C/325F/Gas Mark 3.
Place the chicken in a roasting tray and sprinkle with the cracked black pepper and parsley stalks. Pour the wine and the water over the chicken. Cook for thirty minutes until gently cooked.
Allow to chill and use as required.

Caesar Dressing:

2oz/50g anchovies, finely diced
3 cloves of garlic
6oz/175g mayonnaise
3oz/75g grated parmesan cheese

Add the anchovies, garlic and mayonnaise to a large mixing bowl, mix well, then fold in the finely grated parmesan. Season and chill.

To assemble the salad: Wash and dry the lettuce and tear it into a large mixing bowl. Add the bacon lardons and the crispy garlic croutons. Mix in a couple of tablespoons of the Caesar dressing and mix well until all the lettuce leaves are lightly coated in dressing. Transfer to individual serving bowls, top with sliced, oven-poached chicken and scatter with the freshly-grated parmesan.

Slow-Roasted Tomato & Courgette Galette   Serves 6-8

This is a delicious option to have for a vegetarian as it is bursting with both flavour and colour. Basically, this is an open tart on puff pastry. The word 'galette' is a French term to describe any flat and freeform open tartlets, cakes and so on.

1 sheet of ready-rolled puff pastry
Approximately 6 ripe plum tomatoes
1 large courgette
3 cloves of garlic, chopped
1 tablespoon olive oil
3 tablespoons spiced autumn fruit chutney
(p 143), basil pesto or black olive tapenade

Approximately 7oz/200g brie cheese, sliced
Salt & freshly-ground black pepper

To glaze:
1 egg, lightly beaten

Preheat the oven to 190C/375F/Gas Mark 5.
Slice the courgette and halve the tomatoes.
Place the courgette and tomatoes on a large baking tray with the chopped garlic, drizzle with the olive oil and season lightly with some salt and cracked black pepper.
Bake for 45 minutes until softened.
Remove from the oven and allow to cool.
Place the rolled pastry onto a greased baking tray and pierce several times with a fork to limit the pastry rising.
Brush the pastry with a lightly beaten egg and bake in the oven for approximately 20-25 minutes until risen and golden brown.
When the pastry comes out of the oven press it down with another baking tray to ensure it is completely flat.
Allow to cool down.
Spread the crisp pastry with the chutney, pesto or tapenade, neatly arrange the slow-roasted vegetables on top and then dot in slices of the cheese here and there.
Pop the galette under the grill to heat it a little and to melt the cheese
Drizzle again with some olive oil and serve immediately.

Edward's Top Tip:
If your oven is large enough, the pastry and courgette mixture can be cooked in the oven at the same time.

Baked Flat-Cap Mushrooms with Pine Nut Stuffing & Buffalo Mozzarella Serves 6

This makes a delicious starter or quick supper option. Feel free to vary the type of cheese you use. The beauty of this recipe, if using it for a dinner party is that you can have the mushrooms prepared in advance and then just pop the baking tray into the oven as required

6 large flat-cap mushrooms
2oz/50g butter
1 shallot
1 clove garlic
2 tablespoons freshly-chopped mixed herbs
(parsley, sage, thyme, oregano, chives etc)

1 tablespoon pine nuts
4oz/110g fresh white breadcrumbs
2 balls buffalo mozzarella
2 beef tomatoes, sliced
Salt & freshly-ground black pepper

Preheat the oven to 190C/375F/Gas Mark 5.
Line a flat baking sheet with some baking parchment.
Peel the flat-cap mushrooms and remove the stalks so as to allow for filling.
Arrange the flat-cap mushrooms on a flat baking sheet

Melt the butter and sauté the diced shallot and garlic in the melted butter until soft.
Add the pine nuts, fresh herbs and breadcrumbs.
Allow to cool.
Season the mushrooms with a little salt and pepper.
Put a slice or two of tomato on top of each mushroom.
Cover the tomato slices with a generous portion of the pine nut stuffing and then top with a slice of the buffalo mozzarella.
Bake for fifteen minutes, until the mushrooms are cooked and the stuffing has become nice and crispy.
Serve immediately with a green salad and a little garlic mayonnaise.

Edward's House-Style Pizza   *Makes 2 Pizzas*

You will never again buy frozen pizza after this! Vary your fillings as much as you like.

10oz/300g strong baker's flour
1oz/25g fresh yeast or 1 x 7g sachet of easy blend dried yeast
½ teaspoon of salt

200-250ml hand-hot water (lukewarm, approximately 37C, body temperature)
1 dessertspoon of olive oil

Add the strong flour, yeast and salt to a large mixing bowl.
Mix the lukewarm water and the olive oil together and add to the flour.
Mix the dough thoroughly and then move it out onto a floured surface and knead it for 4-5 minutes or until it feels light and springy under your hands.
Transfer to a clean bowl and cover loosely with a clean cloth.
Leave it to rise for about 30-40 minutes or until the dough has doubled in size.
Preheat the oven to 200C/400F/Gas Mark 6.

Lightly grease two 9inch/23cm flat, round baking trays with a little olive oil.
Once the dough has risen, transfer the dough to the work surface and roll it out into the shape of your desired tin or tins. Spread the dough on the tray and transfer to the oven to bake for about ten minutes. After the ten minutes the dough will have risen slightly and will lift easily off the baking tray. Remove the pizza base(s) from the oven and pile high with a selection of the following toppings: (choose as many as you like, but don't add them all at once!)

Toppings:

7oz/200g tomato passata
3oz/75g fresh pineapple
6 slices pancetta
2oz/50g baby leaf spinach
2oz/50g green or black olives
3oz/75g feta cheese, cubed
1 small tin of anchovies
1 small red onion, sliced

6-8 mushrooms, sliced
1 green pepper, chopped
3oz/75g chorizo, sliced
3oz/75g bacon lardons
2 tablespoons sweetcorn
1 small courgette, sliced
12 cherry tomatoes
6oz/175g grated mozzarella cheese

Transfer to the oven and bake for a further 15-20 minutes until the cheese is bubbling and everything is well cooked through.

Edward's Top Tips:
I normally cook both bases for the preliminary ten minutes, then I allow one to cool down, wrap it tightly in clingfilm and freeze it for a later 'pizza date'. If you like pizzas with a thinner base you should divide the dough between three baking trays.

Spaghetti with Slow-Roasted Tomatoes & Lemon Cream   *Serves 4-6*

I think it's nice to make an extra effort when cooking for vegetarians. This particular recipe is a favourite of mine to whip up when I come in from work in the evening as it is super quick and tasty. Sometimes, if I had some in the fridge, I might also throw a little Parma ham or smoked chicken into the pan.

24 cherry tomatoes
½ tablespoon sunflower oil
12oz/350g spaghetti
1 onion, finely diced
3 cloves garlic, finely diced
½ green chilli, very finely diced
4 large flat cap mushrooms, sliced
1 courgette, sliced into slices

3floz/75ml/½ glass wine
5floz/150ml pouring cream
Zest of 1 lemon
1 tablespoon chopped flat leaf parsley
Salt & freshly-ground black pepper
4oz/110g grated parmesan cheese

Preheat the oven to 150C/300F/Gas Mark 2.
Place the tomatoes onto a flat baking tray or roasting dish.
Drizzle with a small amount of oil and season lightly with salt and pepper.
Place in the oven and roast for 1 hour.
Remove from the oven and leave to cool down
Meanwhile bring a large saucepan of lightly salted water to the boil.
Add in the spaghetti and cook according to the packet instructions.
In a separate wide based sauté pan heat the oil and add the onion, garlic and chilli, sauté on a low heat for 2-3 minutes. Add in the sliced mushrooms and courgettes and continue to cook gently for a further 2-3 minutes until they too have softened down. Next pour in the white wine and allow this to bubble up and reduce by half. Pour in the cream next and allow the mixture to come to the boil. Season lightly with salt and pepper.
Drain the spaghetti and add this to the cream mixture.
Next add in the slow roasted tomatoes, lemon zest and the chopped parsley.
Toss lightly to ensure that everything is mixed thoroughly.
Add in half of the grated parmesan cheese and mix well.
Season lightly with salt and cracked black pepper and ensure that everything is piping hot.
Transfer to serving dishes and sprinkle with the remaining parmesan.
Serve with some crisp garlic bread.

super soups

Roasted Butternut Squash Soup with Smoked Bacon Lardons   Serves 6-8

This is a delicious soup; the smoked bacon lardons give it quite an unusual finish. You could serve it in a china cup, quite a quirky way to serve it for a dinner party or family lunch – it will definitely be the toast of the party! It's ideal to have prepared in advance and is very suitable for freezing.

1oz/25g butter
1 large butternut squash, peeled and chopped
A little oil for roasting
2 carrots, peeled and chopped
1 leek, sliced
2 sticks celery, chopped
1 large sweet potato, peeled and diced
½ medium onion, diced

3 cloves of garlic, crushed and chopped
½ red chilli (optional)
2 pints/1200ml chicken or vegetable stock
3floz/75ml pouring cream
Salt & freshly-ground black pepper

Garnish:
4oz/110g smoked bacon lardons
1 tablespoon natural yoghurt

Begin by preparing the garnish for the soup: heat a large frying pan and cook up the diced bacon lardons on the dry pan until they are crispy. Drain them on kitchen paper and store in a bowl until required.

Preheat the oven to 190C/375F/Gas Mark 5.

Place the chopped butternut squash on a large baking tray, drizzle with a little oil, season lightly with salt and pepper and roast in the oven for 20-25 minutes until it has softened slightly. This will help to add great flavour to the soup.
Select a large saucepan and slowly melt the butter.
Add in all of the carrots, leeks, celery, sweet potato, onion, garlic and chilli; mix thoroughly and continue to sweat them for 6-8 minutes. Continue to keep a constant stir on the vegetables to prevent them from sticking to the saucepan.
Season lightly at this stage with a little salt and pepper and add in the pre-roasted butternut squash.

Next, add in the cream and about two-thirds of the stock. Bring this mixture to the boil and then reduce the heat to a constant simmer. Simmer for the next 15-20 minutes or until all of the vegetables have softened.
Blitz the soup until smooth, adjusting the consistency with the remaining stock as required.
Taste the soup and season accordingly. Those who are more daring may wish to add in some dried chilli flakes at this stage!

Transfer the soup to the serving cups and garnish with the crisp bacon lardons and a drizzle of natural yoghurt.

Slow-Roasted Tomato & Basil Soup Serves 8

Autumn tends to yield large crops of tomatoes, which is great because I absolutely adore tomato soup. Freezing the tomatoes to retain for soup making is a good option, rather than seeing them all go to waste. This particular way of cooking the soup makes for a beautiful flavour and with the addition of the basil it works wonderfully.

1 tablespoons sunflower oil
10-12 medium-sized ripe plum tomatoes, halved
3 garlic cloves, finely chopped
Pinch light brown sugar (optional)
Salt & freshly ground black pepper
1 small onion, finely chopped

2 sticks celery, chopped
2 medium potatoes, peeled and cubed
1 level teaspoon tomato purée
1½ pints/800ml chicken or vegetable stock
2floz/50ml pouring cream
2 tablespoons fresh basil, chopped
1 tablespoon natural yoghurt, to serve

Preheat the oven to 170C/325F/Gas Mark 3.
Place the halved tomatoes onto a large roasting tray with the chopped garlic. Season the tomatoes lightly with salt, pepper and brown sugar (if using) and place in the oven to roast for 45 minutes, or until they have softened. This will help to get a really developed flavour into the tomatoes.

Meanwhile, in a large saucepan heat the oil over a gentle heat and add the onion, celery and diced potatoes and cook gently for 5-6 minutes until they have softened slightly. Next add in the tomato purée and the roasted tomatoes and garlic and mix thoroughly.

Pour in the chicken or vegetable stock together with the pouring cream and allow the mixture to come to the boil. Reduce to a gentle simmer and cook for approximately twenty minutes until everything has softened down. Blitz with a hand blender to a smooth purée.
Season to taste with salt and cracked black pepper and add in the chopped basil.

Transfer the soup to warmed cups or bowls and drizzle with a little natural yoghurt.

Curried Celeriac Soup *Serves 6-8*

Soup is a great recipe to have to hand for home entertaining as it can be made in advance and just heated up as required. For dinner parties I like to add a burst of intense flavour to an early course to get the taste buds tantalised and this soup is ideal! Celeriac is a very underrated and under-utilised root vegetable and it makes a very flavoursome soup.

1oz/25g butter
2 large potatoes, peeled and diced
2 sticks of celery, chopped
1 head celeriac, chopped roughly (make sure to remove tough outer skin)
1 medium-sized onion, chopped

2 cloves of garlic, diced
½ green chilli, diced
1 inch/2.5cm ginger, peeled and diced
1 rounded teaspoon Thai green curry paste
2 pints/1200ml chicken/vegetable stock
Salt & freshly-ground black pepper

Heat the butter in a large saucepan and toss in the potatoes, celery, celeriac, onion and garlic together with the diced chilli and ginger. Allow them to cook very gently (and without colour) for 8-10 minutes or until the smallest vegetables are beginning to soften.
Stir in the curry paste and allow this to infuse with the vegetables.

Next start to add the chicken or vegetable stock (approximately ¾ of the stock would be sufficient at this stage) and bring the mixture to a slow boil and then reduce the heat and simmer for an additional 15-20 minutes or until all of the vegetables, including the potatoes, have softened down completely.

Using a hand blender, blitz the soup until it is nice and smooth. If you would like a thinner soup, now is the best time to add any additional stock or cream to thin it down. Correct the seasoning with salt and pepper at this stage.

Reheat the soup gently, transfer to warmed serving bowls and serve immediately.

Apple & Parsnip Soup *Serves 6-8*

This delicately-coloured soup is a most unusual combination of flavours and is a real favourite with my family and friends. Like all the soups in this section, it freezes very well for those of you who are 'effective freezers', that is, those of you who remember to take things back out of the freezer!

1oz/25g butter
4 parsnips, peeled and chopped roughly
2 medium-sized cooking apples, peeled and chopped roughly
1 leek, sliced
1 stick celery, chopped

1 large potato, peeled and diced
1 medium onion, peeled and diced
½ tablespoon honey
1¾ pints/1 litre vegetable stock
3floz/75ml pouring cream
Salt & freshly-ground black pepper

Select a large saucepan and slowly melt the butter.
Add in the parsnips, apples, leeks, celery, potatoes, onion and mix thoroughly to coat them all with a little butter.
Increase the heat under the vegetables and continue to sweat them for the next 10-12 minutes or until the smaller vegetables have softened. Stir the vegetables constantly to prevent them from sticking to the saucepan. Season lightly at this stage.
Retain the high heat under the saucepan, then add in the honey and allow this to sizzle a little.
Add in the cream and the vegetable stock and allow the entire mixture to come to the boil and then reduce the heat to a constant simmer.
Simmer for the next 15-20 minutes or until all of the vegetables have softened.

Blitz the soup until smooth, adjusting the consistency with the remaining stock.
Taste the soup and season with salt and pepper.
Serve in warmed bowls.

Edward's Top Tip:
If you wish you can add a teaspoon of curry paste to the mixture to create a spicier version of the soup. Coconut milk can be used instead of cream, as can fromage frais or natural yoghurt for those seeking a healthier option.

Colcannon Soup Serves 6-8

This is a delicious prepare-ahead option for any occasion. It's a great winter warmer and freezes very well, so you can store any leftovers for another day.

4-6 large potatoes (approx 1½lb/700g)
1 leek
2oz/50g butter
½ medium sized onion
2 cloves of garlic, chopped roughly
3 large sprigs of thyme
2oz/50g shredded cabbage
Salt & freshly-ground black pepper

2 pints/1200ml chicken/vegetable stock
3½ floz/100ml pouring cream

Garnish:
1 teaspoon sunflower oil
4oz/110g smoked bacon lardons/approx 6 rashers smoked bacon

Heat a large pan and dry fry the bacon bits until they are well cooked and crispy. Drain them on kitchen paper and keep them in a bowl until required.

Meanwhile peel and chop the potatoes and add them to the chopped leeks, onions, cabbage and garlic in a large bowl.

Heat a large saucepan with the butter and toss in all of the vegetables together with the thyme sprigs. Allow them to cook very gently (and without colour) for 8-10 minutes or until the smaller of the vegetables are glazed off.

Next add in the chicken or vegetable stock, and mix in the cream and bring the mixture to a slow boil and then reduce the heat and simmer for an additional 15-20 minutes or until all of the vegetables including the potatoes have softened down completely.

Using a hand blitzer, blitz the soup until it is nice and smooth. If you would like a thinner soup, now would be the best time to add any additional stock or cream to thin it down. Correct the seasoning with salt and pepper at this stage also.

Transfer it to your serving bowls or cups and garnish the soup with crispy bacon lardons and an optional sprig of thyme if you so desire.

Serve as required or alternatively allow the soup to cool down and then transfer it into suitable containers and freeze until required.

Edward's Top Tip:
I normally add about two thirds of the stock at the start and use the rest to correct the consistency at the end.

Pea & Broccoli Soup *Serves 6-8*

In a restaurant environment 'green' soups tend not to be as popular as the orange coloured ones, but this particular soup is one of my personal favourites. It is very rich so a small portion is sufficient.

½ tablespoon sunflower oil
1 large onion, chopped
4 cloves of garlic chopped
2 potatoes, peeled and chopped
1¼ lb/600g frozen peas
14oz/400g broccoli, broken into spears

1¼ pint/700ml chicken stock
5floz/150ml pouring cream
Salt & freshly-ground black pepper

Garnish:
1 tablespoon natural yoghurt

Add the oil to a large saucepan and sweat the chopped onions, garlic and potato for a moment or two.
Add in the frozen peas to the saucepan and mix those around for a moment of two before adding the broccoli.
Now add in a pinch of salt and some cracked black pepper.
Next pour in the chicken stock and the pouring cream and bring the mixture to a rapid boil. Reduce the heat and simmer for 12-15 minutes until the peas have softened, yet still retain their green colour.
Using a hand blitzer or food processor, blitz in batches until the soup is smooth.
Return the mixture to a clean saucepan, correct the seasoning and reheat gently.
Serve piping hot and garnish with a swirl of natural yoghurt.

'Get Better Soon' Chicken Soup *Serves 6-8*

When you are sick and feeling miserable there is nothing like a big bowl of chunky chicken soup to help put the pep back in your step! This recipe is a great way of using up leftover roast chicken, particularly from the leg and the thighs, which in most homes tend to be the last remaining items left on a roast chicken after Sunday lunch. As this soup is a broth-style soup it is essential to have all the vegetables chopped into small bite-size pieces.

1 tablespoon sunflower oil
1 red onion, diced
3 cloves garlic
1 inch root ginger, chopped finely
½ green chilli, very finely diced
2 sticks celery, diced in small, bite-size pieces
1 leek, diced in small, bite-size pieces
2 large potatoes, diced in small, bite-size pieces

2 carrots, diced in small, bite-size pieces
2 pints/1200ml well-flavoured chicken stock
12 cherry tomatoes
14oz/400g cooked chicken, shredded into strips
4-5 stems spring onions, chopped
2 tablespoons flat leaf parsley, chopped

Heat a medium-sized saucepan with the oil and add the diced red onion, garlic, ginger and chilli and sauté on a very low heat for 2-3 minutes and then add the diced celery, leek, potato and carrot and continue to cook for a further moment or two until the vegetables are all glazed. Season lightly with a little salt and pepper.

Next add in the chicken stock and cherry tomatoes and allow the mixture to come to the boil.

Reduce the heat to a gentle simmer and then add in the shredded chicken.

Continue to cook until the vegetables are all softened. About five minutes before serving mix in the chopped spring onions and the chopped flat leaf parsley, then taste the soup to ensure you are happy with the overall taste. Adjust the seasoning if necessary or add some additional stock if you would like a thinner consistency. Serve immediately with some crusty bread.

Edward's Top Tip:
Although this recipe suggests that you serve the soup as a broth, you can of course choose to blitz the soup and serve as puréed soup.

not just your daily bread

Cheese & Onion Soda Bread

This bread is a really nice alternative to the traditional white soda bread. It stays fresh for 3-4 days and also freezes quite successfully. I have suggested other flavours so you can choose one to best suit yourself. Flavourings are always added in before the buttermilk as they are easier to incorporate at this stage.

1lb/450g plain white flour
1 level teaspoon of bread soda
½ teaspoon of salt
12floz/350ml buttermilk, approximately

Flavourings:
1 medium onion
6oz/175g cheddar cheese, grated

Preheat the oven to 170C/325F/Gas Mark 3.
Grease a 9inch/23cm round baking dish.
Heat a little oil in a small saucepan and sweat the onion until just softened.
Allow to cool.
Sieve the plain flour and bread soda into a large mixing bowl.
Add in the salt at this stage also.
Add in the softened onion and the grated cheese.

Pour in the buttermilk and mix until a soft, sticky dough has been achieved.

Transfer the dough onto a well-floured work surface and knead until the dough has been manipulated into a round shape.
Press into the previously prepared tin, dust the top of the bread with a little flour.
Using a sharp knife, cut a cross in the top of the bread and pop into the oven to bake.

Bake for forty-five minutes in the tin and then invert the bread and pop it back into the tin upside down and bake for an additional 5-10 minutes to firm up the crust on the underneath.

ADDITIONAL FLAVOURS:	SUGGESTED AMOUNTS:
Garlic & rosemary	2 cloves garlic, 2 sprigs of rosemary
Sultanas soaked in orange juice	3oz/75g
Roasted vegetables	1½ mixed peppers, ½ red onion, ½ courgette
Curry, apricot & red chilli	2 dessertspoons curry powder, 6 apricots, pinch chilli flakes
Grated mozzarella	3oz/75g
Bacon & thyme	5-6 rashers of bacon, lightly grilled, 2 stems thyme
Cheddar cheese & rocket	2oz/50g cheese, 2 dessertspoons chopped rocket
Sundried tomato & chorizo	3oz/75g sundried tomatoes, 2oz/50g diced chorizo

Multi-Seed Wholemeal Scones *Makes 8-10*

These make ideal lunchbox fillers and freeze exceptionally well; if desired, you can leave out the seeds for plain, wholemeal scones. For a delicious lunch, I sometimes spread these with some citrus crème fraiche (p 156) and top with smoked salmon.

8oz/225g extra coarse wholemeal flour
8oz/225g self-raising flour
1 rounded teaspoon baking powder
Pinch salt
2oz/50g brown sugar
2oz/50g hard butter, cut into cubes

4oz/110g mixed seeds (pumpkin, sunflower, poppy, sesame etc)
1 egg
7floz/200ml buttermilk (approx)

Egg wash:
1 egg, beaten with 2 tablespoons of milk

Preheat the oven to 190C/375F/Gas Mark 5.
Place the wholemeal flour into a large mixing bowl and sieve the self-raising flour and baking powder into it.
Add the sugar and the salt.
Rub in the butter with your fingertips until it resembles rough breadcrumbs.
Mix in 3oz/75g multi-seed mix.
Add in the egg and buttermilk and mix well until the mixture comes together, adding a little extra buttermilk if required.

Turn the mixture out onto a lightly-floured work surface, knead, then flatten out slightly and, using a scone cutter, cut the dough into approximately 8-10 pieces.
Brush the tops of the scones lightly with egg wash and place on a greased tray.
Sprinkle the remaining seeds over the top and bake for 18-20 minutes.
When baked the scones will be well risen and golden brown, and when lifted will come away easily from the tray and feel very light.

These additional ingredients can be added:
Leftover bacon pieces
Sundried tomatoes
Grated cheese
Mixed herbs
Walnuts/pinenuts

Pumpkin Seed Bread

This is ideal for a dinner party as you can have all of the dough prepared in advance. The main difference between yeast breads, and soda breads is that yeast breads, like this one, take much longer to make because of the rising time allocated before actually baking the bread. This bread is suitable for freezing.

7oz/200g strong white flour
7oz/200g extra-coarse wholemeal flour
1 level teaspoon salt
1oz/25g brown sugar
1 sachet (approx 7g or 1 level dessertspoon) fast-action yeast

12floz/350ml (approx) hand-hot water
2 tablespoons pumpkin seeds
Egg wash:
1 egg beaten with 2 tablespoons of milk

Sieve the strong white flour and salt into a large mixing bowl.

Add in the wholemeal flour and give them a good mix around.

Add the dried yeast sachet and the sugar.

Pour your water into a large jug. (The water should be 37 degrees; hand hot or lukewarm)

Mix the water into the flour mixture and stir well until the mixture has somewhat come together.

Transfer the mixture onto a lightly-floured (with strong flour) surface and knead for 4-5 minutes or until the mixture feels soft and springy to the touch.

Transfer this dough into a large bowl and cover with cling film or with a cloth, leave in a warm place for about an hour or until the mixture has doubled in size.

Meanwhile preheat the oven to 190C/375F/Gas Mark 5. Grease a 9inch/23cm round springform/cheesecake tin. After the dough has doubled in size, break it into small relatively uniform pieces and roll them into little balls or bread rolls.

Arrange them loosely around the springform tin and again leave them in a warm place for an additional half an hour, covered loosely with a clean tea towel.

Make up an egg wash with some egg and milk and brush this all over the top of the bread.

Sprinkle with pumpkin seeds and bake for thirty minutes until well risen and hollow sounding underneath.

To serve, either leave on the table and allow everyone to break the rolls or cut like a cake.

Edward's Top Tip:
If you wish you can make this bread with all strong white flour.

Edward's Brown Bread

One of the most popular recipes in my first cookery book, *Edward Entertains*, was the walnut & treacle bread. Brown bread, of any variety, is always popular so I decided to slightly edit the walnut & treacle version and give you my wonderful recipe for truly magnificent brown bread. Aside from the wonderful taste, this bread is super simple to make, which just adds to the appeal!

14oz/400g coarse wholemeal flour
2oz/50g plain flour
2oz/50g porridge oats
Pinch salt
2 very level teaspoons bread soda

2 large eggs
1 dessertspoon of sunflower oil
18floz/500ml buttermilk

Preheat the oven to 170C/325F/Gas Mark 3.
Place the wholemeal flour into a large mixing bowl.
Sift in the plain flour and the bread soda.
Add the salt and porridge oats into this mixture and mix well.
In a separate bowl beat the eggs together with the oil, then make a well in the middle of the dry ingredients and pour in the egg and oil mixture.
Incorporate the buttermilk and get the mix to a 'sloppy' consistency.
Pour into a well-greased 2lb/900g loaf tin, smooth the top with a wet spoon and sprinkle the top of the bread with some additional porridge oats.
After about an hour in the oven, remove the bread from the tin, turn upside down and pop the upside down bread back in; return to the oven to bake for a further 15-20 minutes.
Remove from the oven and allow the bread to cool down before cutting.

Edward's Top Tips:
Two tablespoons of treacle added to the wet mix makes for darker & sweeter bread.
This bread stays fresh for 4-5 days and can be successfully frozen.
To make individual brown breads, the mixture can be spooned into muffin tins and baked for approx 25-30 minutes at 180C.
If you are nervous that the bread won't come out of the loaf tin when cooked, place a strip of parchment paper across the middle of the tin before pouring in the mixture. When the bread is baked, you can use the parchment to ease it out, if problems arise. Sometimes a sharp tap on a flat surface works a treat also!

Sundried Tomato & Parmesan Plait

This is a very flavoursome bread and looks extremely impressive for a dinner party. It can also be baked as little muffins or bread rolls.

8oz/225g strong white flour
8oz/225g wholemeal flour
Pinch of sugar
Pinch of salt
Freshly-ground black pepper
10floz/275ml (approx) warm water
2oz/50g fresh yeast

2 teaspoons tomato purée
4oz/110g sundried tomatoes, chopped
3oz/75g Parmesan cheese, grated
Sea salt
Egg wash:
1 egg beaten with 2 tablespoons milk

Put the flours, salt, pepper and sugar in a mixing bowl and mix thoroughly.
Combine the yeast with the warm water (again the water should be approximately 37 degrees, so as to activate the fresh yeast).
Don't add all the water to the yeast at once as, depending on the moisture of the tomatoes, it may be moist enough; add about three-quarters of the liquid first and check the consistency as you go along before adding the remaining liquid. Mix well until combined, then whisk the tomato purée into the mixture.

Add this liquid to the flour mixture together with the grated cheese and chopped sundried tomatoes.

Mix until completely combined and knead together on a lightly-floured work surface for a few minutes. Transfer to a clean bowl and cover with cling film or a clean linen cloth.
Leave to rise for about an hour until doubled in volume and then knock the mixture back with your fist.
Again, on a lightly floured work surface, knead the dough lightly until it feels springy to the touch.
Divide the dough into three pieces and roll each shape into a long cylindrical shape.

Press the three ends together and tie up in a French plait (right over centre, left over centre and so on; the centre coil changes each time).
Arrange neatly on a baking tray and leave in a warm place again for about twenty minutes until the shape fills out a little. In the meantime, pre-heat the oven to 190C/375F/Gas Mark 5.
Brush lightly with egg wash and sprinkle with a pinch of sea salt.
Bake for about 25-30 minutes until cooked.

Edward's Top Tips:
You can use dried yeast (2 x 7g sachets) in this recipe instead of fresh. The most obvious difference between the two types of yeast, in terms of the production of the bread, is that the dried yeast is added directly to the flour, whereas the fresh yeast needs to be dissolved in water.
In this recipe, I would suggest dissolving the fresh yeast in approximately 7floz/200ml water first and adding this to the mixture as, depending on the texture and moisture content of the sundried tomatoes, you may not need the full content of water, and if you do it is easier to add the remaining water gradually and as required.

mouthwatering meat dishes

Fillet of Beef & Spring Onion Potato Cakes with Roast Shallot & Balsamic Reduction Serves 6

Beef is always a crowd pleaser and this simple, but tasty recipe will be a big hit. Both the sauce and the potato cakes can be made up in advance, which is a good time saver on the evening of a dinner party.

Spring Onion Potato Cakes:
1 bunch spring onions
4 large potatoes, peeled, cooked and mashed
1 tablespoon fresh parsley, chopped
1 tablespoon of plain flour
1 egg

Preheat the oven to 190C/375F/Gas Mark 5.
Thinly slice the spring onions and mix them with the mashed potatoes, chopped parsley and flour. Beat in the egg.
Mould the mixture into six potato cakes and shallow fry on a hot pan with a little oil until brown on either side, then place them in the preheated oven for a further ten minutes to heat through.

Fillet of Beef:
6 fillet steaks (approx 7oz/200g per person)
Freshly-ground black pepper

Meanwhile heat a large pan with a little oil. Season the steaks with a little black pepper.
Add the steaks to the hot pan and, providing they are not too thick, cook them in the following pattern:
Rare: two minutes on either side
Medium: four minutes on either side
Well done: five minutes on either side

Roasted Shallot & Balsamic Reduction:
2 shallots, very finely diced

1oz/25g brown sugar
5floz/150ml balsamic vinegar

Add the thinly-sliced shallots to a medium-sized saucepan with a tiny amount of oil.
Add the sugar when the shallots have coloured a little.
Allow the sugar to melt, thus caramelising the shallots and then pour in the balsamic vinegar.

Allow this to boil and reduce to a syrupy sauce.
Serve each steak on top of one of a spring onion potato cake and drizzle with the roasted shallot & balsamic reduction.

Homemade Pork Sausages *Serves 6-8*

This is my slightly 'poshed up' version of bangers and mash. There is such a difference when you make your own homemade sausages – their flavour is far superior to the shop-bought alternative.

Sausages:
1lb/450g minced pork
6/8 dried apricots, finely diced
3-4 stems spring onions, finely chopped
2 cloves garlic, finely diced
1 teaspoon fresh sage, chopped

2 tablespoons fine breadcrumbs
1 teaspoon mustard (Dijon, wholegrain etc)
1 egg yolk
Salt & freshly-ground black pepper
½ teaspoon cayenne pepper (optional)
A little plain flour for dusting

Mix the apricots, spring onions, sage and garlic together and add them to the minced pork.

Mix in the breadcrumbs, egg yolk and mustard and season lightly with a little salt and pepper (sometimes I use cayenne pepper for an added kick!)

Flour your work surface with a little plain flour, on it divide the mixture into 6-8 pieces and roll out into cylindrical shapes. I normally place the rolled sausages into the fridge at this stage just to ensure that they stay in shape when you cook them.

In a large frying pan, heat a little oil and cook the sausages on both sides for 5-6 minutes, or until they are cooked through (cut them in the middle to ensure that there are no traces of pink, undercooked meat left); pork needs to be cooked fully through before you serve it.

An alternative way of cooking the sausages is to place them on a lined baking tray and bake in a hot oven (190C/375F/Gas Mark 5) for approximately twenty minutes, until they feel firm to the touch and no traces of pink undercooked meat are left.

Serve with some mashed potatoes flavoured with wholegrain mustard and a little apple and pear chutney (p 144).

Stuffed Pork Chops with Cider & Wholegrain Mustard Gravy _Serves 6_

This is a nice way to cook pork chops, which can sometimes be perceived as a dry offering. You can also use this stuffing for different cuts of meat, like chicken, pork steak or lamb.

6 thick-cut pork chops
1 tablespoon of oil
6oz/175g fresh white breadcrumbs
3oz/75g butter
½ medium onion

2 tablespoons selection of fresh mixed herbs (parsley, thyme, rosemary, sage, chives etc)
4-5 dried apricots, chopped roughly
4-5 dried prunes, chopped roughly

Preheat the oven to 170C/325F/Gas Mark 3
To make the stuffing, melt the butter in a pan, add the onion, apricots and prunes and sweat them without allowing them to colour for 5-6 minutes. At this stage, add the freshly-chopped mixed herbs and combine with the nice, fresh breadcrumbs.

Season the mixture and allow it to cool completely.
Using a sharp knife, split a pocket in the pork chops and stuff some of the fruity stuffing into each one.
Transfer the chops to a roasting dish, drizzle with one tablespoon of oil and bake for 35-45 minutes or until the meat is nice and tender.

Gravy:
1 tablespoon plain flour
½ pint/300ml apple cider

½ pint/300ml chicken stock
1 dessertspoon wholegrain mustard
1 teaspoon chopped sage (optional)

Remove the chops from the roasting tray and place the tray (containing the remaining pork juices) on direct heat on the hob.
Add in the flour and stir gently for a moment, incorporating the juices on the tray.
Slowly whisk in the cider and chicken stock and continue to whisk until the mixture thickens.
Strain through a fine sieve into a clean saucepan and

continue to simmer for ten minutes.
Whisk in the wholegrain mustard and chopped sage (if using).
Pour the gravy over of the stuffed pork chops and serve with some of the cheesy leek and potato gratin (p 96) and some crisp green vegetables.

Herb-Stuffed Leg of Lamb, Rosemary & Redcurrant Gravy   Serves 6-8

A roast joint of meat is one of my favourite things to prepare at home. When we were young, Mum always spent a lot of time preparing Sunday lunch; her preparations always started on Saturday evening as she steeped the peas and made her delicious trifle. I think a traditional Sunday roast holds very special memories for everyone, there is a great sense of family about it.

1 leg of lamb (approx 2kg/4½ lbs) (Ask your butcher to bone and butterfly the leg of lamb.)
Approximately 3 sprigs of rosemary

Stuffing:
3oz/75g butter
½ medium sized onion, diced

1 eating apple, diced
2oz/50g walnuts, crushed or broken (optional)
2 tablespoons of freshly-chopped herbs (parsley, thyme, rosemary, sage etc)
7oz/200g breadcrumbs
Salt & freshly-ground black pepper

Melt the butter in a medium-sized saucepan and use it to gently soften the onion.
Add the eating apple, walnuts and herbs. Continue to cook for a moment or two. Finally, add in the breadcrumbs together with a little salt and freshly-ground black pepper and mix well until combined. Allow to cool completely.
Place the lamb onto a large chopping board, cover with some cling film and use a rolling pin to beat it a little to flatten it out. Ensure your stuffing is cold, then put it in the centre of the lamb and roll the meat up to secure the stuffing inside.
This can be done with some string or you can use a

couple of skewers to secure it in place.
Preheat the oven to 190C/375F/Gas Mark 5.
Using a sharp knife make a number of incisions to the fat of the lamb and stick sprigs of the rosemary in the fat. Season lightly with a little salt and pepper, drizzle with a little oil and roast in the oven for an hour and a half, turning over half way through.
After the first forty-five minutes reduce the oven temperature to 170C/325F/Gas Mark 3 for the remainder of the cooking. Remove the skewers or string at this interval.
Allow the meat to rest for approximately twenty minutes prior to carving.

Rosemary & Red Currant Gravy
1 tablespoon plain flour
3floz/75ml/½ glass red wine
18floz/500ml well-flavoured

lamb/chicken/beef stock
1 teaspoon chopped rosemary
1 dessertspoon redcurrant jelly.

Remove the joint of meat from the roasting tray and place the tray on direct heat.
Add in the flour and whisk until the mixture becomes dry and lumpy in consistency.

Slowly whisk in the red wine and chicken stock.
Strain through a fine sieve into a clean saucepan, add in the redcurrant jelly and chopped rosemary and continue to cook for ten minutes. Serve drizzled over the lamb.

Spicy Beef Fajitas with Cajun Potato Wedges Serves 6-8

This recipe is delicious and so suitable for informal entertaining of family and friends; I like to leave all the components of the meal in the middle of the table and allow the guests to help themselves and build their own fajitas, which can be fun and messy in equal measure! The stir-fry part of this recipe is also suitable for pork, duck or chicken. Here, I have given you the recipe for a number of the classic fajita accompaniments and in its entirety it makes for good family food. I'd advise preparing the wedges first, as they take longest to cook.

Beef Stir-fry Mix:
1 red chilli, very finely chopped
2 cloves of garlic, chopped
1½ lb/700g beef, cut into very thin strips
1½ mixed peppers, thinly sliced
1 medium onion (red or white, thinly sliced)
5-6 mushrooms, sliced
3oz/75g mangetout
3oz 75g baby corn
½ teaspoon of ground cumin
4 tablespoons sweet chilli sauce
Salt & freshly-ground black pepper

Crème Fraiche Spread:
6floz/175ml Crème Fraiche
Juice and zest of 1 lime

Cracked black pepper
1 tablespoon coriander/parsley, freshly-chopped

Guacamole:
1 ripe avocado
1 dessertspoon of chopped coriander/flat leaf parsley
Juice of ½ lemon
¼ red chilli, chopped very finely
Pinch of salt & pepper
½ small red onion, diced
2 plum tomatoes, deseeded and diced,
2 dessertspoons of mayonnaise (optional)

Other Requirements:
7oz/200g grated red cheddar cheese
8-12 medium-sized flour tortillas

It's so simple to make the crème fraiche spread – just mix all of the ingredients together until combined. Chill in the fridge until required.

To make the guacamole, add all ingredients except the tomatoes, red onion and mayonnaise to a food processor or large mixing bowl and blitz (using a hand-held blender if desired) until a relatively smooth purée has been achieved. Remove from the blender and, using a spoon, mix in the mayonnaise (if using), diced red onion and chopped tomatoes. Chill well before serving.

When making the stir-fry element of this dish, you should have all of the ingredients prepared in advance because you do need to stand over this dish while it cooks.

Heat a large saucepan or wok, then add a little oil, together with the chilli, garlic and sliced beef.

Allow the beef to seal off quite quickly. Next add the sliced vegetables, the mangetout and baby corn and allow these to cook quickly for approximately five minutes on a high heat. (See 'TOP TIP')

When the beef and vegetables are almost fully cooked, add the sweet chilli sauce and allow to cook for a further 2-3 minutes, then sprinkle in the ground cumin.

Taste and, if necessary, correct the seasoning of the dish at this stage.

Serve immediately with tortilla wraps, dips and Cajun potato wedges.

Cajun Potato Wedges:

6 large rooster potatoes,
well washed and dried
1 dessertspoon Cajun spices
1 tablespoon oil

Preheat the oven to 190C/375F/Gas Mark 5.
Wash some rooster potatoes and cut into chunky wedges.
Drizzle with the oil and Cajun spice, mix everything together in a bowl and place on a baking tray lined with parchment.
Bake for 35-40 minutes until crispy on the outside and well-cooked through to the centre.
Place all ingredients in the middle of the table and let people help themselves.

Edward's Top Tip:
Refrain from adding any additional oil even if your mixture is dry on the pan, it is better to use some water or stock and partially steam everything. This helps to keep your stir-fry from becoming greasy at the end.

Slow Cider-Roasted Loin of Pork *Serves 6*

The lovely combination of the flavours within the spice rub is absolutely fantastic with the slow-roasted loin of pork. The spice rub is also suitable to serve on pork chops or pork fillet and it gives a nice flavour to what can otherwise be a bland piece of meat.

1 large loin of pork (approx 2kg/4½ lb weight)
1 tablespoon oil

Spice Rub:
2 sprigs of thyme, woody stems removed
1 teaspoon of wholegrain mustard
1 tablespoon honey

1 tablespoon sesame seeds
Grated zest & juice of 1 orange
5-6 black peppercorns
½ teaspoon sea salt

Additional Ingredients:
10floz/300ml apple cider

Take your large loin of pork and, using a sharp knife, score the skin in a criss-cross pattern.
Preheat the oven to 200C/400F/Gas Mark 6.
Put all of the ingredients for the spice rub into a pestle and mortar and crush, or better still pop them into a food processor and blitz until a chunky consistency has been achieved.
Spread the spice rub onto the meat and rub or massage it into the skin of the pork, making sure that it gets down into the incisions that you have made in the skin of the pork.

Gravy:
1 tablespoon plain flour
1pint/600ml chicken stock

Remove the joint of meat from the roasting tray and place the tray (containing the remaining cider and pork juices) on direct heat. Add in the flour and whisk until the mixture thickens. Slowly whisk in the chicken stock.

Put the pork into a deep roasting tray and drizzle with a little oil. Roast for approximately 30-35 minutes in a hot oven.
Reduce the heat to 150C/300F/Gas Mark 2.
Remove tray from the oven, pour the cider over the meat, sprinkle with the sesame seeds, then cover the tray with tin foil and roast for an additional hour and a half.
Allow the pork to rest for at least 10-15 minutes when it comes out of the oven and serve with braised red cabbage (p 89) and roast potatoes (p 97).

1 teaspoon wholegrain mustard
1 teaspoon sage, chopped

Strain the gravy through a fine sieve into a clean saucepan and continue to simmer for ten minutes.
Add in the wholegrain mustard and the teaspoon of chopped sage and serve drizzled over the pork.

Breaded Bacon Chops with Parsley Sauce Serves 6

Bacon chops are chops that are cut from the loin of bacon. This particular way of cooking the chops is extremely tasty and it also works very well with pork chops.

6 bacon chops
1oz/25g plain flour
Salt & freshly-ground black pepper

1 egg beaten with 3 tablespoons milk
6oz/175g fresh white breadcrumbs
1 tablespoon parsley, chopped

Prepare three bowls:

1: Flour seasoned with the salt and pepper

2: Egg and milk whisked together

3: Breadcrumbs with chopped parsley.

First, coat the bacon chops in the seasoned flour, then transfer them to the egg and milk mixture and finally coat them in the breadcrumb mixture, making sure they

are completely coated.
Preheat the oven to 180C/350F/Gas Mark 4. Line a flat baking tray with a little baking parchment.
Heat a large pan with a little oil. Pan fry the bacon chops for 2-3 minutes on each side until golden brown and then transfer to the lined baking tray. Bake in the oven for a further 20-25 minutes.

Parsley Sauce:
1 pint/600ml milk
2oz/50g butter
2oz/50g flour

3floz/75ml/½ glass white wine
2 tablespoon parsley, freshly-chopped
Salt & freshly-ground black pepper

Put the milk in a saucepan and bring to the boil.
In another small saucepan, melt the butter slowly. Add in the flour and mix until combined.
Cook this mixture on a low heat for two minutes to take the taste of the flour away.
Gradually whisk in the boiling milk and the white wine and continue to stir, especially around the edges, until it comes to the boil again. Then turn the heat right down and cook on a low heat for 10-15 minutes. Just before serving, add the chopped parsley and season.

Edward's Top Tips:
If you would like the parsley sauce a little thinner you can whisk in some additional hot milk/water/stock.
The sauce also freezes quite well and it can be flavoured with lots of different items like herbs, cheese, mushrooms, wholegrain mustard etc.

something fishy

Chilli-Crusted Monkfish   Serves 6

The flavoured crust on this gives a wonderful kick. This is an ideal dish to cook if you like to have things prepared in advance. Be warned this is a hot option!!

6 portions monkfish
About 18 cherry tomatoes
(preferably on the vine)
1 lime, cut into wedges

Chilli Crust:
2 red chillies (seeds retained –
some like it hot)
2 cloves of garlic
Pinch of cayenne pepper
Juice of 1 lime
2 stems of spring onions, chopped
2 large dessertspoons of oil

This is so simple – just put all the ingredients for the chilli crust into a food processor and purée until they have come together into a soft paste, then spread over the monkfish. You can allow the fish to marinade for 4-6 hours, but if you're tight for time a few minutes is sufficient as the crust is so well flavoured.
Preheat the oven to 190C/375F/Gas Mark 5.
Arrange the monkfish on a baking tray (I normally line the baking tray with a little parchment paper first) and scatter the cherry tomatoes and lime wedges around.
Transfer to the oven and bake for 17-20 minutes depending on how thick the pieces of fish are; when cooked the fish should be firm to the touch.

Serve the monkfish with some basmati rice (cooked as per the packet instructions), a large salad and the roasted cherry tomatoes and lime wedges.

Edward's Top Tips:
This chilli crust can be used on most types of fish; it is particularly good on cod or salmon.
The chilli-crusted monkfish is also delicious when served cold and I often use it as part of a cold buffet.
Why not use the chilli crust as a marinade for chicken breasts prior to cooking them on a barbecue?

Blackened Salmon with Spiced Couscous Salad & Citrus Yoghurt Dressing *Serves 6*

People are always looking for a way to liven up salmon, well look no further!

Blackened Salmon:

6 salmon fillets

2 level teaspoons Cajun spice

1 tablespoon chopped fresh mixed herbs

(parsley, mint, thyme, oregano)

1 tablespoon oil

Zest of 1 lime

2 whole chillies, roughly chopped (optional)

half a lemon, cut into wedges

In a small bowl mix together the Cajun spice, chopped mixed herbs and the oil. Add in the lime zest and the salmon fillets and mix well.

Leave the salmon to marinate in the fridge for twenty minutes.

Preheat the oven to 190C/375F/Gas Mark 5.

Line a baking tray with some parchment paper.

In a large pan, heat a little oil and pan-fry the salmon flesh side down for 2-3 minutes to give the flesh a nice 'blackened' effect.

Remove the salmon from the pan and place on the lined baking tray. Sprinkle the tray with some roughly-chopped chillies (if using) and lemon wedges and bake in the oven for approximately a 15-18 minutes, or until the salmon feels firm to the touch.

Spiced Couscous Salad:

7oz/200g couscous

Approximately 14floz/400ml boiling water

3oz/75g sultanas/currants

1 small courgette, grated

1 small carrot, grated

16 cherry tomatoes, halved

4 stem spring onions/scallions, chopped

3oz/75g dried apricots, diced

2oz/50g walnuts, chopped

Zest & juice of 1 lemon

½ teaspoon chilli flakes

½ teaspoon ground cumin

3 tablespoons oil

2 tablespoons mint, chopped

Salt & freshly-ground black pepper

Place the couscous in a large mixing bowl and cover with boiling water and then cover with a clean cloth.

Leave to stand for ten minutes and then fluff it up with a fork. Allow it to cool down for about half an hour.

When the couscous has cooled, add in all remaining ingredients and mix together well.

Season lightly with salt and black pepper and store in the fridge until required.

Citrus Yoghurt Dressing:

8floz/225ml natural yoghurt

Juice of 1 lime

1 tablespoon mint, freshly-chopped

Cracked black pepper

In a small bowl mix, together the yoghurt, lime juice, freshly chopped mint and the black pepper. Store in the fridge until required.

Assembly: Place the couscous onto a large serving plate and arrange the salmon fillets on top.

Drizzle generously with the citrus yoghurt dressing and serve immediately.

Deep Fried Plaice & Chips with Creamed Peas Serves 4

Fish, chips and mushy peas – though we hate to admit it we all love it! I prefer this method of coating the fish to a thick batter, which can be too heavy – it often seems that there's more batter than fish. Plaice is a very versatile fish and this is just one way to use it. If you wish, you could use other types of fish, such as John Dory, cod or haddock for this dish. I have also included a method for cooking the perfect chip!

Edward's Thick-Cut Chips
4 large potatoes (roosters/maris pipers)

Sunflower/vegetable oil for deep frying

Peel the potatoes and cut into thick pieces.
Heat the oil in a deep fat fryer. Test it by dropping a piece of bread into the oil; if it's sufficiently hot the bread will crisp up in 30 seconds.
Once the oil is hot drop the chips into it and cook until they are almost fully cooked. At this stage lift the chips up from the oil, allow the oil to heat back up for 2-3 minutes and carefully drop the chips back into the hot oil for 2-3 minutes until they turn nice and crisp.
Drain well on kitchen paper and store in the oven for a remaining 3-4 minutes whilst you are cooking the fish.

Deep Fried Plaice:
4 large fillets of plaice
1 egg
2floz/50ml milk
1oz/25g seasoned flour (plain flour with salt and pepper)
5oz/150g breadcrumbs
1 tablespoon sesame seeds
1 teaspoon of chilli flakes

Remove the skin from each fillet of plaice.
Prepare three bowls:
1: Seasoned flour
2: Egg wash mixture: egg and milk whisked together
3: Breadcrumbs with sesame seeds & chilli flakes

Dip the pieces of fish in the flour first to coat, shake off the excess and then transfer to the egg wash mixture, coating completely and finally toss the egg-coated pieces of fish in the breadcrumb mixture. Using your hand, gently press the breadcrumbs onto the fillets of plaice. Place on a tray in the fridge to rest while you make your pea purée.

To Cook:
Heat the deep fat fryer with some vegetable/sunflower oil. Check that the oil is hot enough (see Thick-Cut Chips recipe, above).
Carefully drop the coated fillets of plaice (in batches) into the deep fat fryer.
Deep fry the fish until golden brown. This should take no more than 3-4 minutes.
Drain on some kitchen paper and serve immediately.
Serve the fish with creamed peas and home-made chips.

Creamed Peas:
8oz/225g frozen peas
2 cloves of garlic, finely diced
½ medium sized onion, finely diced

4 mushrooms, thinly sliced
4floz/110ml cream
1 tablepoon mint, freshly-chopped
Salt & freshly-ground black pepper

In a large saucepan quickly fry off the onion, garlic and mushrooms until lightly browned.

Add in the frozen peas and allow to cook gently with onion, garlic & mushroom mixture for 3-4 minutes.

Add in cream and cook until the peas have softened and the cream has reduced and thickened slightly (allow no more than 5 minutes).

Mix in the freshly chopped mint at this stage.

Correct the seasoning and serve immediately.

Edward's Top Tip:
The different elements of this dish all cook in a relatively short period of time so it is worth spending a little extra time preparing all different elements and then cook them all almost simultaneously. Start by cooking the creamed peas and the chips. The fish only takes a few minutes to cook, so this is normally the last item I start on. Trust me, it is well worth the effort!

Chilli Crab Salad with Smoked Salmon *Serves 6*

In recent years Thai cuisine, and Thai-influenced cuisine, has become very popular in Ireland. This salad fuses some quintessential Thai ingredients with fresh crab meat. Crab is a very tasty shellfish; though it is often described as 'poor man's lobster', in my opinion its flavour is far superior! It's also a very good source of protein, which is essential for the body's growth and repair.

6 slices smoked salmon
Mixed lettuce leaves

Chilli Crab Salad:
1lb/450g fresh crab meat
½ red chilli
Juice of ½ lemon or lime
Black pepper
2 tablespoons crème fraiche
1 tablespoon coriander, chopped

Place all the crab meat in a large bowl and, with the tips of your fingers, check carefully to make sure that all pieces of shell have been removed, as they can be quite sharp. (For convenience, I normally wear disposable gloves when checking the crab).

Dice the chilli very finely (in case you are the person to get the big piece!), then add it, with the chopped coriander and the crème fraiche, to the crab meat and season with the lemon or lime juice and cracked black pepper.

Mix thoroughly and correct the seasoning to suit your own taste.

You can serve this in a variety of ways:

1. Lay the salmon out flat on the plate, place a spoon of the crab salad on the side and serve with some mixed lettuce leaves and a slice of brown bread.

2. To make a smoked salmon and crab parcel, line a ramekin with smoked salmon, pile the crab salad in on top and then close the edges of the salmon over the crab. Invert this from the ramekin onto a plate to make an attractive-looking parcel.

3. Spoon small quenelles of the mixture onto circles of toasted soda bread as very attractive canapés.

4. Spoon the crab meat into an unfluted scone cutter or tian ring (available from all good kitchen shops) and top with a thin layer of very smooth guacamole (p 54).

5. Use as part of a starter 'seafood and shellfish tasting platter' with smoked salmon, lime & ginger calamari, tempura prawns and smoked trout paté.

Smoked Haddock Baked in Fennel Cream   Serves 4

This particular dish is a really satisfying and filling option to serve on top of some creamy cheesy mashed potatoes. It is comfort food at its best.

4 fillets smoked haddock
1 small fennel bulb, chopped into chunks
4 mushrooms, sliced
1 dessertspoon flour
10floz/300ml milk

2floz/50ml cream
1oz/25g butter
1oz/25g grated cheddar cheese
1 dessertspoon chives, freshly-snipped

Preheat the oven to 190C/375F/Gas Mark 5.

Choose a shallow casserole dish and line it with a piece of baking parchment.

Fold the haddock fillets in three and place them in the casserole dish.

Meanwhile, heat the butter in a large pan, add the fennel chunks and mushrooms and sauté gently for a few minutes until they are softened completely. Add the flour and coat everything in the pan with it. Next, pour in the cream and milk and allow to come to a gentle boil.

Pour this mixture over the smoked haddock in the shallow casserole dish and scatter the cheese on top.

Cover the casserole dish with a layer of tinfoil or a tight-fitting lid and bake in the oven for fifteen minutes, until the fish is nice and flaky and is sitting in a thickened sauce.

Sprinkle the snipped chives over the top and serve immediately.

one pot wonders

Chicken Jambalaya   Serves 6

One-pot wonders are very popular now as people have become so 'time-poor'. This particular dish is one of my favourites and I often whip it up for impromptu get-togethers. Basically it's a great way of using up any bits and pieces you have lying around. I like it quite spicy, as is often the case with Cajun cookery, but you can adapt it to your own taste.

1lb 8oz/700g chicken breasts, diced
½ teaspoon cayenne pepper
1 tablespoon sunflower oil
4oz/110g chorizo, sliced
4oz/110g smoked bacon lardons
1 large onion, diced
4 cloves garlic, crushed
1 green pepper, diced
2 sticks celery, chopped

1 green chilli, diced finely
8oz/225g basmati rice
14oz/400g tinned chopped tomatoes
1 pint/600ml well-flavoured chicken stock
2 tablespoons flat-leaf parsley, chopped
Tabasco sauce, to taste
Cracked black pepper

Begin by putting the raw chicken pieces into a bowl with the cayenne pepper and the oil and mixing well. If time allows you can leave this chicken to marinate for about twenty minutes, or better still overnight.

Heat a little oil in a wide-based sauté pan, then add the chicken pieces and cook for 3-4 minutes on a high heat until browned all over. Next add the chorizo and the bacon lardons and continue to cook for a further few minutes until the chorizo has coloured the chicken.

Prepare the onions, garlic, celery, chilli and green pepper now, add these to the pan with the chicken and reduce the heat to a lower setting.

Cook for 3-4 minutes until the vegetables have begun to soften, then add the uncooked rice and mix well to ensure that it's fully incorporated throughout the dish and coated with all the flavourings.

Next, pour in the chopped tomatoes and the stock and allow the mixture to come to the boil.

Secure with a tightly-fitting lid.

Allow to simmer for approximately twenty minutes, giving the mixture an occasional stir during that time and adding in a little additional stock if the dish is becoming too dry.

Finish with the freshly-chopped parsley and season to taste with some Tabasco sauce and cracked black pepper.

Serve immediately.

Chilli & Prawn Risotto *Serves 6*

People can often be nervous or intimidated by risotto recipes, but in my 'Top Tip' I have given you a stage at which you can have the risotto partially cooked in advance of the soirée.

1oz/25g butter
1 tablespoon oil
1 shallot, peeled and finely diced
1 red chilli, very finely diced
2 cloves garlic, crushed finely
1 stick celery, peeled and finely diced
Approximately 12-18 prawns
9oz/250g arborio (risotto) rice

3floz/75ml/½ glass dry white wine
1 pint/600ml pints chicken/fish/vegetable stock, boiling
2floz/50ml cream (optional)
2oz/50g freshly-grated Parmesan
Salt & cracked black pepper
1 tablespoon parsley or coriander, freshly-chopped

In a large wide-based sauté pan, heat a little butter and oil.

Finely dice the shallots, chilli, garlic and celery into small pieces and sauté until softly cooked. Next add in the Arborio rice and sauté this gently allowing it to mix with the softened vegetables. Pour in the wine and allow it to evaporate off.

Then you need to start adding in the stock, little by little: add a ladleful of boiling stock, stir gently and when the rice has absorbed the liquid, then add in a little more. Repeat this process until the rice is almost fully cooked (be conscious of the fact that you may not need all the stock in the recipe, the best way to determine if the risotto is sufficiently cooked is to taste it).

When the risotto is almost fully cooked you can add the cream and the prawns. Allow the prawns to cook fully (this should take about 3-4 minutes) and then add in some chopped fresh parsley or coriander to the dish.

Serve with a rocket salad.

Edward's Top Tip:
When adding in the stock, ensure that you add it very slowly and this will make for a delicious risotto. Adding it all in at once can make for a very stodgy risotto.
Risotto, in theory, does not reheat very well but once the rice is almost fully cooked (and before you add the cream & the prawns) if you wish, you can transfer the mixture to a flat baking tray and stir for a few minutes to assist the mixture in cooling down and then put it aside until you need to carry on with the rest of the cooking at a later stage.

Huevos Rancheros *Serves 4*

Welcome to Mexico with this traditional brunch option! It is absolutely delicious and is lovely to serve to friends who have stayed over after a dinner party. It is particularly well received if joyful night has been followed by sorrowful morning!

1 tablespoon of oil
1 courgette
1 red onion
½ red pepper
½ green pepper
1x 14oz/400g tin of tomatoes (fresh plum tomatoes could also be used)
6-8 mushrooms, sliced
4 cloves of garlic, crushed
1 teaspoon fresh oregano or thyme, chopped
4 large free range eggs
Salt & freshly-ground black pepper

Slice all of the vegetables into small evenly-shaped pieces.
Gently heat a shallow, wide-based pan.
Add oil to the pan and fry the vegetables and crushed garlic until they are all glazed and beginning to soften.
Pour in the chopped tomatoes (or fresh if you prefer) and the oregano or thyme and allow the mixture to cook very gently on a nice, low heat for about ten minutes.
Make four hollows in the mixture and crack an egg into each. Place a lid on top of the pan and allow to cook on a gentle heat for 4-5 minutes, until the eggs have firmed up.
Season lightly and then serve with some warmed pitta breads or tortillas.

Chicken, Leek & Wholegrain Mustard Bake With Potato Topping   *Serves 6*

This is a quirky variation to the traditional creamed potato topping. Without the potato topping this dish is delicious mixed through some hot pasta or served with boiled rice or creamed potatoes.

1oz/25g butter
½ tablespoon oil
4 large chicken fillets, diced
4 rashers of smoked bacon or 4oz/110g bacon lardons
2 medium-sized leeks, sliced thinly
6 mushrooms, sliced
3 cloves garlic, crushed
1oz/25g plain flour
2 dessertspoons grated cheddar cheese

3floz/75ml/½ glass white wine
14floz/400ml milk
2floz/50ml pouring cream
1 teaspoon wholegrain mustard

Topping:
5-6 large potatoes, scrubbed well
1oz/25g fresh white breadcrumbs
1oz/25g grated cheddar cheese
Salt & freshly-ground black pepper

Put the potatoes into thick slices, put them into a large pot of salted water and bring to the boil.
Cook for 8-10 minutes, until the potatoes are tender but not fully cooked through.
Strain into a colander and allow to cool.
Meanwhile, heat the butter (and the oil to stop the butter from burning) in a large, shallow saucepan.
Add the chicken and smoked bacon and cook for 4-5 minutes, then add the leeks, garlic and mushrooms, together with a little seasoning.
After a further five minutes, sprinkle in the flour and use this to dry up any liquids in the pot and to thicken the sauce.

Pour in the white wine, grated cheese and milk and allow the mixture to come to a gentle boil, stirring all the time. Add the cream now also. Season lightly and add the wholegrain mustard.
Simmer for 5-6 minutes and then transfer to a large casserole dish.
Preheat the oven to 190C/375F/Gas Mark 5.
Neatly arrange the sliced potatoes on the top, sprinkle with some salt, pepper, cheese and breadcrumbs and bake for approximately half an hour.

Peppered Beef Casserole   Serves 6-8

This casserole-style dish is perfect for all the family to enjoy! Also it is quite a rich dish so it would be a perfect treat for a winter dinner party.

A little butter and oil for frying
2lb/900g diced stewing beef
2 large onions, diced
10-12 button mushrooms
2 carrots, diced
1 green pepper, diced
Garlic (4 cloves, chopped)

Fresh herbs (rosemary & thyme)
1 large tablespoon of plain flour
1 teaspoon tomato purée
1½ pints/800ml beef stock
3 tablespoons brandy
7floz/200ml cream
1 tablespoon cracked black peppercorns

Preheat the oven to 150C/300F/Gas Mark 2.

Heat a little butter and oil a large pan and quickly brown off the meat until it is browned all over. Cook in batches if necessary; make sure not to do too much meat at once, because the meat will begin to stew as opposed to brown off. Transfer the meat to a large casserole dish.

Add the diced carrots, onion, mushrooms, garlic and green peppers to this pot after cooking the meat. Add a sprig or two of rosemary and thyme. Scatter the plain flour and the crushed black peppercorns over the ingredients and mix well over a low heat. Don't worry about the flour browning off at this stage; this will only help to further colour and develop the flavour of the sauce. Slowly pour in the brandy and beef stock and continue mixing with a wooden spoon to combine the flour with the liquid and to thicken the sauce.

Bring the sauce to the boil and allow to boil for 4-5 minutes. Stir in the tomato purée and the cream; taste the sauce and correct the seasoning if necessary.

Pour the sauce into the casserole dish over the meat and cover with a tight-fitting lid. Transfer to the oven for approximately 2½ -3 hours. Don't forget to take the dish out of the oven every so often (perhaps every hour or so) and give it a stir to make sure that the liquid has not evaporated. If it has you will need to add a little more beef stock. I normally remove the lid for the last 15-20 minutes of the cooking time.

After the cooking time has been reached bring the entire casserole dish to the table and sprinkle it with some chopped parsley. I like to serve this with baby boiled potatoes dressed with butter and chopped parsley, or with a large chunk of bread and a glass of a good, full-bodied merlot.

Edward's Top Tip:
Tinned chopped tomatoes can be added to the dish instead of the cream as a lighter option.

Fragrant Chicken Serves 6

This dish consists of lightly-marinated chicken served in a rich, creamy and lightly-spiced curry sauce.

Chicken Marinade:

4 chicken breasts
2 cloves garlic
5 tablespoons yoghurt
½ teaspoon chilli powder
1 tablespoon fresh coriander, chopped
½ teaspoon turmeric

Fragrant Sauce:

½ tablespoon oil
1 medium onion, sliced
2 red chillies
2 cloves garlic
1 tin chopped tomatoes (14oz/400g)
½ teaspoon each cayenne pepper, ground coriander, ground cumin, turmeric
7floz/200ml pouring cream/natural yoghurt (or even a combination of both)
Fresh basil or coriander, chopped, to garnish
1 pinch crushed chilli flakes (for the more daring!)

Cut the chicken into large chunks.

Mix the chopped garlic with the yoghurt, chilli powder, fresh coriander and turmeric.

Mix the diced chicken into this yoghurt marinade and leave it for at least an hour – longer if time allows (yoghurt marinades can even be left overnight).

Heat a little oil in a large, heavy-based frying pan. Add the marinated chicken and brown lightly.

To make the sauce, blitz the chillies, onions and garlic in a food processor or with a hand-held blender until they are coarsely chopped. Add these to the pan also and allow them to cook for a few moments and then add in the chopped tomatoes and additional spices. Continue to simmer for 5-10 minutes before finally adding the cream/yoghurt and simmering for a further 12-15 minutes.

Garnish with freshly-chopped basil or coriander.

Correct the seasoning, adding some of the crushed chilli flakes if desired.

Serve with rice or naan bread.

Edward's Top Tips:
This is a great prepare-ahead meal.
The chilli flakes can be added with the chopped tomatoes for added kick.

Oven-Baked Beef Cobbler _Serves 8_

This is a real winter warmer, perfect for those dark winter days. If you want to cook this in its entirety on the range without the cobbler topping feel free to do this also. Sometimes I would use a creamy potato topping instead (much like a cottage pie) and this also works wonderfully well. As with all slow-cooked dishes it is delicious on the next day as well. It takes a bit of time to prepare, but it is definitely worth the effort.

2oz/50g butter
½ tablespoon oil
2 medium onions, diced
3 cloves garlic, diced
2lb/900g stewing beef, cut into cubes
8oz/225g button mushrooms, sliced or quartered
2oz/50g plain flour
Tiny pinch cayenne pepper/smoked paprika

800ml/1½ pints well-flavoured beef stock, approx
3floz/75ml/½ glass red wine
1 bay leaf
3-4 sprigs of fresh thyme
1 tbsp tomato purée
1 tbsp Worcestershire sauce
Salt & ground black pepper

Heat the butter and a little oil in a large saucepan over a gentle heat and add the diced onion and garlic and sweat them off for 3-4 minutes until lightly softened.

Add the diced beef to the mixture and quickly seal the meat all over. Cook in batches to ensure the meat gets properly browned. Once the beef has browned (approx 4-5 minutes) add the button mushrooms together with a little salt and pepper. Cook for a further moment or two.

Next, mix the flour with a little cayenne pepper and add this to the beef mixture in the saucepan; use it to coat all of the beef and vegetables – this will give a fluffy, dry coating to the contents of the saucepan. Don't worry about the flour browning off, this will just give a good colour to the sauce later on.

Meanwhile, bring the beef stock to the boil and then gradually pour it into the beef mixture in the saucepan, stirring continuously until the sauce begins to thicken. Add in the red wine, tomato purée, bay leaf, thyme sprigs and Worcestershire sauce and allow the entire mixture to come to the boil. Once it's boiling, reduce the heat and simmer for 1½-2 hours until the beef is tender.

Preheat the oven to 190C/375F/Gas Mark 5.

Transfer the entire mixture to a large casserole dish and allow to cool slightly while you make the topping.

Topping:
12oz/350g plain flour
1 rounded teaspoon baking powder
Pinch salt
3oz/75g butter, diced
2oz/50g cheddar cheese, grated
10floz/300ml buttermilk

1 teaspoon of dried, mixed herbs or 1
dessertspoon of freshly-chopped herbs
½ teaspoon cayenne pepper or paprika
1 large egg
Egg wash:
1 egg beaten with 2 tablespoons milk

Sieve the flour, baking powder and cayenne pepper into a large bowl.
Add the salt and diced butter. Gently rub the butter into the flour.
Add the grated cheese and mixed herbs.
In a separate bowl, lightly whisk the egg and add to the dry ingredients.
Mix in the buttermilk to achieve a soft, sticky dough.

Using a little extra flour roll the dough into a large piece and using a small scone cutter cut out rounds of about 1½ inches thick and press on top of the beef casserole mixture.
Brush lightly with the egg wash; you can also sprinkle with a little extra cheese if you wish.
Bake in the oven for twenty-five minutes.
Serve with some boiled potatoes and green vegetables.

Sweet & Sour Pork with Pineapple Serves 6

This sweet and sour sauce, which I make separately and add to the pork stir-fry mix, will last for three or four days in the fridge. It also freezes well, so you can have a batch ready in the freezer to whip up a quick and delicious meal.

I use cornflour as a thickening agent in this recipe; it is used quite a lot in oriental cookery. The flavour of the homemade sauce is far superior to anything you'd get in your local take away! The addition of the pineapple works wonderfully with the pork – and the little bit of fruity acidity aids digestion. Instead of pork, you can use beef, chicken, duck or prawns for an equally tasty dish.

Sweet & Sour Sauce:
1 tablespoon soft light brown sugar
2 tablespoons rice vinegar/white wine vinegar
2 tablespoons sherry
4floz/110ml dark soy sauce

175ml/6fl oz chicken stock
2 tbsp tomato ketchup/chilli jam
1 lightly-rounded dessert spoon of cornflour mixed with a little water
Dash of Tabasco sauce (optional)

Put the sugar, vinegar, sherry, soy sauce and chicken stock into a medium-sized saucepan with the tomato ketchup/chilli jam. In a separate bowl mix the cornflour with a little water to make a paste and add this to the liquids in the pot. Add a dash of Tabasco, if desired.

Bring the entire mixture to the boil, stirring continuously, and then reduce the heat to a simmer for 8-10 minutes until the sauce is of coating consistency. Transfer the sauce to a large jug and use as required.

Pork Stir Fry:
2 tablespoons oil
2 medium pork steaks (trimmed of excess sinew) (Approx 1½lb/700g)
½ inch fresh ginger, finely diced
2 cloves garlic, finely diced
Pinch cayenne pepper
2 tablespoons oil

1 carrot, cut into thin strips
1½ mixed peppers (½ each red, green, yellow), cut into thin strips
1 red onion, thinly sliced
6 button mushrooms, thinly sliced
4oz/110g fresh pineapple, diced or 1 small tin pineapple chunks
Bunch spring onions, chopped

Cut the pork into long strips and sprinkle with the cayenne pepper, diced ginger, garlic and oil. Mix together and, if time allows, leave them to marinate for an hour or so.
Heat a wok or frying pan and cook the pork mixture in small batches until browned all over.
Set the browned pork aside on a plate.
Meanwhile add the peppers, mushrooms, onion and

carrot (cut into strips) to the wok and cook them gently. Return the browned pork to the wok at this stage.
After a further 6-7 minutes, pour in the sweet and sour sauce and bring this mixture to the boil.
Add in the diced pineapple and chopped spring onions just before you are ready to serve.
Serve with some cooked boiled basmati rice.

Fisherman's Pie *Serves 6*

Recipes for fisherman's pie vary greatly, but this is my preferred option. I simply adore coming home from work to this delicious one-pot wonder. Sometimes rather than putting the savoury crumble on top I would just use the seafood mix as the sauce for a seafood pasta or vol-au-vent or for a fisherman's pie topped with mashed potato or puff pastry.

Seafood mix:
1oz/25g butter
1 small head fennel, diced, outer leaves removed
1 potato, diced
1 leek, thinly sliced
1 carrot, finely diced
2 cloves of garlic, crushed
3 sprigs of thyme
1oz/25g plain flour
5floz/150ml/1 glass white wine
12floz/350ml fish stock (p 85), water or mild chicken stock
7floz/200ml pouring cream
1½ lb/700g selection of fish (you could include cod, salmon, smoked fish, prawns, mussels etc. Save the skin for the fish stock (p 85)
½ shot Pernod
Salt & freshly-ground black pepper
1 tablespoon basil or tarragon, freshly-chopped

Savoury Crumble Topping:
8oz/225g breadcrumbs
3oz/75g melted butter
3 dessertspoons of fresh herbs, e.g. parsley & thyme, chopped
2oz/50g flaked almonds
2oz/50g grated parmesan cheese
Zest of one lemon

Begin by making the savoury crumble. This is a very simple topping to prepare – just mix all the ingredients together in a large mixing bowl.

Next dice the vegetables in nice, bite-size pieces and in a deep, wide based sauté pan, sauté them in the butter with the garlic and thyme until they are glazed, but without colour. Scatter in the plain flour and use it to coat the vegetables and dry up all the juices.

Add the white wine and fish stock, together with the cream. Bring to the boil and allow to simmer until the vegetables soften.

When the vegetables are soft add the fish and shellfish. At this stage, try not to stir the mix too much as this will cause the fish to break up.

Cook, very gently, for 5-6 minutes just until the fish is cooked, then season and add in some freshly-chopped basil or tarragon, together with the Pernod.

Transfer to a casserole dish and top with savoury crumble.

Bake in a hot oven (190C/375F/Gas Mark 5) for twenty minutes until the topping is golden-brown and the fish pie is piping hot.

Serve with a large green salad or crisp roast potatoes (p 97).

SIMPLE FISH STOCK:

4oz/110g (approx) skin from the fish

1 stick of celery

3 black peppercorns

1 bay leaf

Several stalks of fresh parsley

1 wedge of lemon.

2 pints/1200ml water

Bring the entire mixture to the boil for 10 minutes.
Drain through a sieve and retain until required.

versatile veg

Braised Red Cabbage *Serves 6*

This is a favourite of mine and I think it works particularly well with roast meats. Although this is a quintessential Christmas dish, I would cook and serve it all year round. The flavour of the star anise gives the dish a really unusual flavour, but it can be relaced with an extra stick of cinnamon if you can't get your hands on star anise.

1 tablespoon sunflower oil
2 medium onions, diced
1 cinnamon stick
2-3 pieces star anise
4oz/110g demerara sugar

1 medium head red cabbage, thinly shredded
2 large cooking apples, cut into chunks
3oz/75g sultanas
4floz/110ml red wine vinegar
10floz/300ml red wine

Heat a little oil in a large saucepan and sweat the onions, cinnamon stick and star anise for 4-5 minutes, until the onions have completely softened. Add in the sliced red cabbage and diced apples and continue to cook for 4-5 minutes until they have begun to soften slightly. Then add in the sugar and all remaining ingredients and put a lid on the saucepan. Cook on a low heat for about an hour and then check to make sure it is cooked – the cabbage should be a very robust claret colour and the majority of the liquids should have reduced.

This dish is lovely the next day, just very gently reheated with a little extra wine.

Edward's Top Tip:
You need to stir this every few minutes to make sure that the liquid has not reduced off too quickly. Add some additional wine if required.

Honey-Roasted Parsnips *Serves 4-6*

The combination of the honey and parsnips works wonderfully.

4 large parsnips
1oz/25g butter
1 tablespoon oil
2 dessertspoons honey
2-3 sprigs of thyme

1 tablespoon sesame seeds
Salt & freshly-ground black pepper

Preheat the oven to 190C/375F/Gas Mark 5.
Peel the parsnips and cut into large, chunky wedges, removing the hard fiberous core.
Place the parsnips in a large pot of salted water. Bring to the boil and allow to boil for 4-5 minutes. Strain off the water.
Place parsnips onto the roasting tray (lined with baking parchment).

Slice the butter onto the parsnips, drizzle with oil, season and break up the thyme stalks on the top.
Roast in the oven for about twenty minutes.
Remove from the oven and drizzle the honey over the roasting parsnips and return the tray to the oven and cook for a further 15-20 minutes until the parsnips are thoroughly cooked and glazed with the honey.
Sprinkle with some sesame seeds just before serving.

Brussels Sprouts with Bacon lardons & Toasted Almonds *Serves 4-6*

This is a delicious way of jazzing up your simple Brussels sprouts.
See top tip for blanching and refreshing for 'Prepare Ahead Vegetables' (p 93) and utilise it whenever you need to.

1 bag of Brussels sprouts (about 18 sprouts)
4oz/110g bacon lardons, preferably smoked
2oz/50g butter

3oz/75g flaked almonds
Salt & freshly-ground black pepper

Trim the Brussels sprouts, taking off the rough outer leaves.
Make a cross with a sharp knife in the bottom of each.
Bring a pot of salted water to the boil and add the sprouts.
Boil for 6-8 minutes until soft and tender.
Strain off the water.
Meanwhile in a large pan or wok melt the butter and quickly fry the bacon lardons until crispy.
Add the sprouts and toss around in the pan making sure that they are well coated and piping hot.
Season with a little salt and pepper and then scatter in the almonds and allow them to toast on the pan for 2-3 minutes.
Serve immediately.

Edward's Top Tip:
If you wanted to make a vegetarian version of this recipe then just proceed with the recipe without using the smoked bacon lardons and when you are adding in the flaked almonds add in 3oz/75g of crumbled blue cheese and allow this to melt into the Brussels sprouts.

Prepare-Ahead Dinner Party Vegetables *Serves 6-8*

This is my absolute favourite way to serve vegetables, particularly for a dinner party or if entertaining a crowd. Although it may seem a little laborious it is well worth the effort. I think one of the most demanding elements of a dinner party is ensuring everything is ready at the same time. This particular dish means you can serve up a large bowl of mixed vegetables, all regenerated at the same time and using only one saucepan – revolutionary! Pay special attention to the 'blanch & refresh' processes (see Top Tip).

2 carrots, sliced into large wedges
1 parsnip, diced
½ turnip, diced
1 small head broccoli, broken into spears

1 small head cauliflower, broken into florets
4oz/110g frozen peas
2oz/50g garlic & herb butter (see below)
Salt & freshly-ground black pepper

Blanch and refresh the carrots, parsnips, turnip, broccoli & cauliflower.
Make sure the vegetables are well dried off.
When ready to serve the vegetables, heat a large pot with the garlic butter.
Add in the blanched and refreshed vegetables together with the frozen peas and sauté gently for 6-7 minutes until they are piping hot.
Season lightly, and as required, and transfer to a large serving bowl.
Serve immediately.

Garlic & Herb Butter:
4oz/110g softened butter

3 cloves garlic, crushed
1 tablespoon, fresh parsley, chopped

In a small bowl combine the softened butter with the garlic and chopped parsley.
Store in the fridge until required.

Edward's Top Tip:
To blanch and refresh:
This is a process by which you cook the vegetables as normal in boiling water and then, just as they are cooked, run them under ice cold water until they have cooled completely.
Strain off the cold water and pat dry with some kitchen paper.
At this stage, you could keep the vegetables in the fridge for up to twenty-four hours.
Try to be very clever when blanching and refreshing the vegetables. For example, the carrots & turnips would take a similar time to cook so they could be cooked and cooled together, as could the broccoli & cauliflower.

spuds-u-like

Cheesy Leek & Potato Gratin _Serves 6_

A delicious way to serve the potato option at a dinner party as you can have it all prepared and just cooking very gently in the oven by the time your guests arrive, which clears space on the stove top. Adding parsnip or celeriac, instead of the leeks, makes for a very interesting taste.

6-8 large potatoes
1 large leek, finely sliced
3 cloves of garlic
1oz/25g butter

10floz/300ml cream
4oz/110g grated cheddar & mozzarella
cheese mix (or your preferred hard cheese)
Freshly-ground black pepper

Preheat the oven to 170C/325F/Gas Mark 3.
Peel and thinly slice the potatoes and leek.
Peel and chop the garlic.
Layer the slices of potato, leek and garlic in an ovenproof dish.
Dot a little butter and sprinkle a little cheese between the different layers, then season with black pepper.
Put the cream into a saucepan and bring to the boil, then pour the cream over the potatoes until they are almost covered. (You may need more or less cream than in the recipe depending on the size of your dish.)
Sprinkle the remainder of cheese on the top.
Cover the dish with a layer of baking parchment and tinfoil and bake for about an hour.
After the hour, remove the tinfoil and bake for an additional 10-15 minutes to allow the cheesy top to get lovely and crisp.

Ed's Crunchy Roasties Serves 4-6

What is it about roast potatoes that we always want 'just one more'?
This is a foolproof way of cooking the potatoes, which keeps them really nice
and crispy on the outside and soft on the inside.

8-12 potatoes (I normally find rooster
potatoes are best for a crunchy finish)

2 tablespoon goose or duck fat
1 tablespoon plain flour

Put the potatoes into a small saucepan, cover with water
and bring to the boil.
Reduce the heat and simmer for ten minutes, until the
potatoes are beginning to soften around the edges, but
are still firm in the centre.
Put the fat onto a roasting tray and place the tray in a hot
oven (190C/375F/Gas Mark 5) for a few minutes to melt.
Strain the potatoes and give them a little shake.
Add the flour to the potatoes at this stage and shake
them around until they are lightly coated.
Add the potatoes to the hot fat and cook for 35-40
minutes, turning occasionally, until crispy on the outside
and tender and fluffy on the inside.

Edward's Top Tip:
If you wish, you could add some cloves of unpeeled garlic
and rosemary sprigs to the potatoes when roasting for a
varied flavour.

Potato Salad with Smoked Bacon & Wholegrain Mustard Mayonnaise Serves 6-8

I love barbecues and this is one of my favourite salads to have at a barbecue. It's not as laden with mayonnaise as some of its counterparts and the flavour of the smoked bacon gives the simple salad a quirky twist. I have included the recipe for the red onion marmalade on p 145, but if you do not have time to make it try substituting another relish, such as mango chutney or sweet chilli jam.

16 baby potatoes
5oz/150g smoked bacon lardons
3 tablespoons red onion marmalade (p 145)
1 bunch spring onions, roughly chopped

1 tablespoon parsley, chopped
1 teaspoon wholegrain mustard
2 tablespoons mayonnaise
Salt & freshly-ground black pepper

Heat a frying pan and dry-fry the smoked bacon lardons until crispy.
Parboil the baby potatoes (in boiling water) for 8-10 minutes until just tender and then allow them to cool in a colander.
Once they are cool, slice the potatoes into rough chunks and place in a large mixing bowl.
Add the bacon lardons, red onion marmalade, spring onions, chopped parsley, wholegrain mustard and mayonnaise to the potatoes.
Mix well and season as required with a little salt and pepper.

Duchess Potatoes *Serves 6*

This is a great dish to have prepared in advance – you can have the potatoes piped out the day before and then just cook them when required. It's also a great way of using up left-over creamed potatoes. You'll need a piping bag for this recipe.

4 large potatoes (I normally use roosters)
2 egg yolks
1 tablespoon parsley, chopped
Salt & freshly-ground black pepper

Egg wash:
1 egg yolk beaten together with 2 tablespoons milk

Peel, boil and mash the potatoes. (Don't use any milk or butter when mashing the potatoes.)

Allow the potatoes to cool slightly, then mix in the egg yolks, salt and pepper and the chopped parsley.

Transfer the mixture to a piping bag (if the mixture is not soft enough to pipe successfully, mix in a little heated milk to correct the consistency).

Preheat the oven to 200C/400F/Gas Mark 6.

Pipe the potatoes into a beehive shape onto a greased or lined baking tray.

Place in the fridge for at least half an hour (or overnight if desired) to allow them to firm up, which will help perfect the shape when you bake them.

Brush with a little egg wash and bake for 12-15 minutes.

sweet temptations

French Lemon Tart   Serves 8-10

Lemon tart is one of those desserts that people always order when they are out in a restaurant and yet never want to make at home, perceiving it to be very difficult to make. There's no need to be afraid of this recipe – it's really quite straightforward.

Sweet Pastry
10oz/300g plain flour
4oz/110g caster sugar
5oz/150g butter
1 large egg

Filling:
7 large eggs
7oz/200g sugar
Zest and juice of 4 lemons
10floz/300ml cream

There are several ways to make the sweet pastry:
In a food mixer: put all ingredients into mixer and mix until bound together.
Wrap in cling film and allow to rest.
By the creaming method: cream the butter and sugar until light and fluffy, add in the egg and flour and bring the mixture together.
Wrap in cling film and allow to rest.
By the 'rubbing in' method: place the sifted flour in a large bowl with the caster sugar.
Rub in the butter with your fingertips until the mixture resembles fine breadcrumbs.
Beat the egg and add to the dry ingredients and bind it together.
Wrap in cling film and allow to rest.
When you have made the pastry, preheat the oven to 180C/350F/Gas Mark 4.
Roll out and blind bake the sweet pastry tartlet shell in a 9inch/23cm flan ring (See 'How to Blind Bake', p 11).
Turn the oven down to 150C/300F/Gas Mark 2.

Place all the ingredients for the filling into a large saucepan over a medium heat and beat continuously until the mixture has thickened (it should take about ten minutes).
Strain the lemon custard into the prepared tartlet shell and bake in the preheated oven for 15-20 minutes.
Allow to chill for at least 2-3 hours, but overnight is fine, and then dust liberally with icing sugar and, using a hot blowtorch or under the grill, glaze the tart until caramelised.
Serve immediately.

Edward's Top Tips:
This sweet pastry is a great kitchen staple. It's wonderful to have in your freezer and can be called on for many of your baking requirements.
If desired, you could pop a little lemon zest into the pastry as well or why not use a mixture of lemon and lime in the filling to make a lemon and lime tart?

White Chocolate Bread & Butter Pudding   Serves 6

This is a twist on a classic dish. It's a wonderful treat to take out of the oven after a traditional Sunday roast; it's so simple to make, which just adds to the appeal. Feel free to leave out the white chocolate, but it does add an extra richness to the dessert.

1 loaf of sliced bread, buttered and crusts removed (approx 12-16 slices)
18floz/500ml milk
3½ floz/100ml pouring cream
7oz/200g caster sugar

5 large eggs
3oz/75g sultanas (See 'Top Tips')
4oz/110g white chocolate
2oz/50g flaked almonds, optional
¼ teaspoon of ground cinnamon

Butter all the slices of bread and cut off the crusts.
Preheat the oven to 180C/350F/Gas Mark 4.
Put the milk and cream into a large saucepan and allow the mixture to come to the boil. Immediately transfer the milk and cream into a jug.
Mix the sultanas with 2oz/50g of the sugar.
Layer the bread in a 9inch/23cm ovenproof dish and scatter the sultana and sugar mix between each layer of bread. You should end up with three (or four) layers of bread altogether with the sultanas scattered in between each. The top layer should be just bread – do not put sultanas on the top, they will burn.
Break the five eggs into a large mixing bowl, add the remaining 5oz/150g sugar and beat together until combined. Then add the white chocolate (chocolate drops or a bar, chopped finely) and the cinnamon.
Pour the hot milk and cream over the egg and chocolate mixture and whisk well until combined. Slowly pour this egg, milk, cream, chocolate mixture over the bread and butter and allow it to stand for about ten minutes to allow the liquid to become absorbed by the bread.
Scatter the flaked almonds on the top of the soaked pudding.
Put into the oven and bake for 40-45 minutes until the pudding is well risen and almost set to the touch.
Serve with butterscotch sauce (p 110) and cream.

Edward's Top Tips:
If you wish you can leave out the white chocolate or substitute dark chocolate.
Sultanas should be rinsed in hot water before use and if you wish (or if time allows) you can soak them for approximately thirty minutes in either orange juice or whiskey for a more developed flavour.
You can have the pudding assembled and soaked in advance and leave it in the fridge until you are ready to cook it. This can be done up to 24-36 hours in advance of cooking.
When cooked, this pudding will keep in the fridge for 2-3 days.

Milk Chocolate Parfait in a Dark Chocolate Shell

Serves 6

Parfait is a beautiful frozen dessert that's lovely to have after a substantial dinner party as it is a light and cooling option. It looks like a very fancy special occasion dessert, and it has the advantage that you can have it made in advance. The direct translation from French means 'perfect' and after you have made and tasted this you will know why! This dish involves making a flavoured Italian meringue, folding in some whipped cream and allowing it to freeze.

Dark Chocolate Shells: 5oz/150g dark chocolate

Melt the dark chocolate in a large bowl set over a pan of simmering water.
Select some silicone, dome-shaped moulds and brush or spread the melted chocolate over the inside of the mould. (If you have any dark chocolate left add it to the milk chocolate when you are melting it for the parfait.)

Make sure that the inside of the mould is completely coated in dark chocolate whilst trying not to have it too thick. Place the mould upside down on a tray or plate and pop into the freezer for a few minutes until you are ready to fill with the parfait.

Parfait:
4oz/110g milk chocolate
2oz/50g caster sugar
1 dessertspoon liquid glucose

4 tablespoons water
2 egg yolks
4floz/110ml cream, lightly whipped

Melt the milk chocolate in a large bowl set over a pan of simmering water.
Meanwhile place the sugar, liquid glucose and water into a small saucepan and bring to the boil, reduce the heat and allow to simmer for 3-4 minutes or until the mixture thickens slightly.
While it's thickening, place the egg yolks in the electric mixer and whip for 4-5 minutes until very pale and creamy.
Reduce the speed of the machine to a low speed and slowly pour in the boiling sugar mixture.
Allow the mixture to beat for 8-10 minutes or until the mixture has cooled down completely.
Add the melted milk chocolate and then gently fold in the softly-whipped cream. Do not over mix at this stage.

Pour the mixture to the prepared chocolate shells and transfer to the freezer for up to twelve hours or overnight.
To serve remove the parfaits from the moulds by simply pressing them out, whilst still frozen.
Leave to sit for about five minutes before serving.

Edward's Top Tip:
If you can't get the dome-shaped moulds that I have used you can use the silicone muffin trays which are so readily available in most large supermarkets and department stores. Also sometimes I have made this parfait (without the shell) by just pouring it into a loaf tin lined with cling film and freezing. When frozen cut into thin slices and serve.

Iced Bakewell Tart *Serves 6-8*

Bakewell tart originates from the Derbyshire town of Bakewell. It is a layer of sweet pastry filled with berry jam, topped with a rich almond frangipane and baked in the oven. There are many variations to it, but the classic is still my favourite.

Base:
1 x quantity of sweet pastry (p 103)
4 tablespoons raspberry or strawberry jam

Frangipane:
4oz/110g butter, softened
4oz/110g sugar
2 eggs
4oz/110g ground almonds
2oz/50g plain flour
½ teaspoon almond essence

Topping:
4oz/110g icing sugar
2 tablespoons hot water (approx)
1oz/25g almonds, toasted and flaked

Preheat the oven to 180C/350F/Gas Mark 4.
Line an 8inch/20cm round, shallow baking tray with sweet pastry.
Spread the berry jam all over the base of the tart.
To make the frangipane:
Cream the butter and sugar until light and fluffy, then gradually beat in the eggs and almond essence.
Sieve the ground almonds with the flour and gently fold into the butter mixture.
Mix gently.
(This frangipane mixture will keep fresh in your fridge for up to one week.)
Spoon or pipe the frangipane all over the jam-covered base of the tart.
Transfer to the oven and bake for approximately half an hour.
(You can check if it is cooked by sticking a skewer into the centre of the cake and ensuring that it comes away clean).

Allow the tart to cool down and then make up the topping:
Mix the icing sugar with the boiled water until a smooth pouring consistency has been achieved. Roughly pour and spread the topping over the tart and sprinkle with toasted flaked almonds.
Allow to set for about ten minutes and then slice and serve.

Edward's Top Tips:
You could substitute some stewed apple or rhubarb for the jam.
Almonds are toasted by placing on a baking tray and baking in a hot oven for approximately ten minutes.

Baked Lemon Pudding with Lemon Syrup *Serves 6-8*

For those who like something sharp and refreshing to finish a meal, this is definitely the option for you! The lemon syrup can be poured over fruit salad as well or used as a moistening agent for rich sponges and cakes.

8oz/225g butter, softened
8oz/225g caster sugar
Zest of 2 lemons
4 large eggs

8oz/225g self-raising flour (or plain flour with 1 teaspoon of baking powder)
1oz/25g ground almonds
1 tablespoon of milk (if necessary)

Preheat the oven to 180C/350F/Gas Mark 4.
Soften the butter and beat in a large mixing bowl with the sugar for 4-5 minutes.
When this mixture is creamy and fluffy add in the eggs, flour and ground almonds.
Mix thoroughly until completely combined, then stir in the lemon zest.
It is important to scrape down the bowl to ensure that all of the butter has been incorporated into the pudding mixture.
The mixture needs to be of dropping consistency. If you find the mixture is a little tight you can add a spoonful of milk to loosen it up.
Divide the mixture between 6 or 8 well-greased individual pudding basins/dariole moulds/ramekins.
Place the puddings onto a baking sheet and bake for 25-30 minutes until a skewer inserted comes out clean.
When they are still hot, lightly press the puddings into shape if they have risen excessively and remove from the tin immediately. They look more attractive served upside down, so pressing down any excessive rising will make them easier to stand on the plate.

Lemon Syrup:
Juice and zest of 2 lemons
9floz/250ml water

3oz/75g caster sugar
1oz/25g butter
1 rounded dessertspoon of cornflour

Place the lemon juice, zest, water and sugar into a small saucepan and bring to the boil.
Meanwhile, dissolve the cornflour in a little water, and when the lemon and sugar mix, is boiling whisk in the cornflour and simmer uncovered for 5-6 minutes, tasting before serving to ensure that the taste of cornflour is gone from the liquid.
Just before serving the sauce, whisk in the butter; this will slightly darken the colour of the sauce and will also give it a beautiful gloss or shine.
Serve the sauce over the steaming-hot puddings.

Edward's Top Tip:
If you would prefer a brighter-coloured sauce you can use one or two drops of good quality yellow food colouring.

Sticky Toffee Pudding with Butterscotch Sauce

Serves 6-8

This is my adaptation of a recipe given to me by a former head chef, Brian Heffernan, who inspired me so much. If you can get your hands on some nice little individual pudding basins then individual puddings are really cute, but if not you can use a regular pudding basin – the large pudding will be just as well received! Take your time making this and ensure that you have all your weighing out done in advance.

Base:
4oz/110g brown sugar
4oz/110g butter
3 eggs
8oz/225g plain flour

1 teaspoon mixed spice
1 teaspoon baking powder
4oz/110g sultanas
2oz/50g golden syrup

Using your electric mixer, cream the butter and sugar together until they are light and fluffy.
Add the eggs, flour, baking powder and mixed spice and beat thoroughly. The mixture, at this stage, will be quite creamy. Add the golden syrup, together with the sultanas, and beat well until thoroughly combined.
Pour the mixture into a well-greased 2 pint/1.2 litre pudding bowl.
Place a greaseproof paper disc on top of the mixture and secure with a tight-fitting lid.
Sit the pudding bowl into a large saucepan half-filled with water and pop a lid on the saucepan.
Bring the saucepan to the boil and then reduce to a low simmer.
Steam lightly for a further 2 hours.
Invert onto a large serving platter and pour some butterscotch sauce on top!

Butterscotch Sauce:
3oz/75g butter

3oz/75g dark brown sugar
10floz/300ml pouring cream

Melt the butter in a medium-sized saucepan and then add in the brown sugar.
Allow the mixture to come to the boil and then whisk in the pouring cream.
Simmer until the sauce is of coating consistency
Serve immediately over the sticky toffee pudding or store in the fridge until required.
This sauce will last in the fridge for up to three weeks.

Edward's Top Tips:
If you are using individual pudding basins to bake the puddings, place them into a deep roasting tray. Fill with water up to halfway up the sides of the pudding basins and cover with a layer of parchment paper and tin foil. Cook in a preheated oven (180C/350F/Gas Mark 4) for 1 hour 15 minutes.

Pear & Almond Tart *Serves 12*

The combination of pears and almonds works very well in this dish. It takes a little bit of work to assemble the entire dessert, but it's very well worth the effort – once it's glazed it gives the real look of a dessert from a French patisserie!

1 quantity sweet pastry (p 103)
Almond Filling:
6oz/175g butter
6oz/175g caster sugar
½ teaspoon of almond essence
3 large free-range eggs
2oz/50g plain flour
6oz/175g ground almonds

Topping:
6-8 canned pear halves (Canned pears work better for this recipe as they tend not to discolour during the cooking process.)
2 dessertspoons of apricot jam

Use the pastry to line a 9inch/23cm loose-bottomed flan ring or tartlet mould.

At this stage I normally like to transfer the flan ring to the fridge for 20-30 minutes to make sure that the pastry is firm; this will prevent shrinkage at a later stage.

Preheat the oven to 180C/350F/Gas Mark 4.

In a large mixing bowl cream the butter and sugar together with the almond essence (this will give it a more intense almond flavour) until it is really light, creamy and fluffy. At this stage add in the eggs and beat well between each addition. Sieve the ground almonds and flour together and add these to the creamy egg mixture.

Pour this mixture into the pastry-lined flan ring until it has coated the entire base; alternatively, you can pipe in the filling.

Carefully slice the canned pear halves thinly (see Top Tips) and place them, round side upwards, on top of the almond sponge mixture, keeping them in their original shape.

Bake in the oven for 35-40 minutes, until the almond filling is cooked and the pastry has become golden brown.

After the tart has cooled sufficiently, remove it from the tin and place it on a serving platter.

Put the apricot jam into a small saucepan with about two dessertspoons of boiling water and bring it to a very rapid boil. Brush the tart with the boiled jam and serve with freshly-whipped cream.

Edwards's Top Tips:
When you are slicing the pears, slice them from ¾-way up the pear to the very bottom.

There's no need to try and push the pears into a fanned position going into the oven because this fanned position will naturally occur when it is baking.

To get a really shiny glaze it is vitally important that the apricot jam is boiling hot.

Peach & Strawberry Pavlova *Serves 6*

I think pavlova is an eternally popular dessert; it's always a great success. Also, for the calorie conscious it does have a considerably lower quantity of fat than other desserts (you might need to go easy on the cream though!)

3 large egg whites
6oz/175g caster sugar
½ teaspoon of cornflour
½ teaspoon of vinegar
½ teaspoon of vanilla extract

To garnish:
Freshly-whipped cream
3-4 peaches
10-12 strawberries

Preheat the oven to 130C/250F/Gas Mark ½.

Choose a large, spotlessly-clean electrical mixing bowl. Put the egg whites into the mixing bowl and whisk them vigorously until they are stiffly beaten – that is to say, if you were to turn the bowl upside down the eggs wouldn't come out of the bowl.

Reduce the speed of the mixer and add the sugar bit by bit until it is all incorporated. It is important to beat well between each addition of sugar.

Next, you need to turn off the mixer and add the vanilla extract, cornflour and vinegar and then return the mixer to full speed for 50-60 seconds.

Using a piping bag, pipe the meringue mixture into six or eight shell-shapes onto a baking tray lined with parchment paper. Place in the oven and after 15 minutes reduce the heat to 110C/225F/Gas Mark ¼ for a further 45 minutes or until the edge of the meringue feels crisp to the touch but the centre will still be quite soft.

Allow to cool completely (preferably overnight) and then decorate with freshly whipped cream and thinly sliced peaches and halved strawberries

Edward's Top Tips:
Leftover meringue nests can be mashed up in a bowl with some whipped cream and sliced strawberries and piled into a fancy glass and served as the quintessentially English 'Eton Mess'.
Instead of piping this mixture out into meringues you could also just spread it into a circular shape and make one large pavlova. No need to vary the cooking time.

Vanilla Crème Brûlée   Serves 6-8

Crème brulée is one of my all time favourite desserts. When made properly it is an absolute joy. I love to serve this dessert for a dinner party because you can have it made up in advance and it really is a great crowd pleaser; the guests won't want to go home!

½ vanilla pod
4 egg yolks

4oz/110g caster sugar
10floz/300ml pouring cream

Preheat the oven to 150C/300F/Gas mark 2.

Scrape the seeds from the vanilla pod.

Put the cream and vanilla (pod and seeds) into a small saucepan and bring to the boil.

Whisk the egg yolks and sugar together until they are light and creamy.

Pour the boiled cream in on the whisked eggs and sugar and whisk well until properly combined. Strain out the vanilla pod.

Allow to rest for a few minutes until the froth settles, or alternatively you can scoop the froth off.

Choose six large ramekins or 8 smaller ones (flat brulée dishes can also be used).

Carefully pour the egg custard into the ramekins.

Place them in a deep roasting tray and fill it with water about 1/3 way up the side of the ramekins.

Cook for approx 40-50 minutes until set, but still retaining a slight wobble.

Allow to cool down and then refrigerate until required.

Sprinkle with a little brown sugar and then pop them under the grill or glaze with a chef's blowtorch and serve.

Edward's Top Tips:

Three other ways to flavour the crème brulée:

You can place some stewed apple, rhubarb or even mixed-berry compote on the bottom of the ramekins before pouring in the egg custard to provide a hidden element.

You can remove an amount of cream (no more than 75ml) and replace it with another liquid to make the total liquid content 10floz/300ml. I have used espresso coffee or Bailey's in the past.

You could replace the vanilla with either 6-8 stems lavender, 2 stalks lemon grass or 2 inches root ginger.

Lemon, Ginger & Passion Fruit Cheesecake   Serves 8-10

I just love the combination of lemon and ginger. Cheesecake is a very popular dish and this particular flavour is superb. You need to be quite careful when making this particular recipe as it can 'over set' with the addition of the lemon, so take your time.

12oz/350g gingernut biscuits
5oz/150g melted butter
8oz/225g cream cheese
1pint/600ml pouring cream
1 packet lemon jelly (135g pack)

3 tablespoons water
7oz/200g lemon curd
2 passion fruit, seeds for garnishing
6floz/175ml whipped cream, to garnish

Place a 9inch/23cm springform tin ring onto a large serving platter.

Break the biscuits into fine crumbs by either placing in a freezer bag and beating with a rolling pin or placing in a food processor.

Pour in the melted butter and mix well.

Press the biscuits into the base of the serving platter in an even layer and allow to chill.

Meanwhile place 3 tablespoons of water in a bowl with the jelly and heat slowly in the microwave until the jelly has melted.

Place the cream cheese and 3oz/75g of the lemon curd into a large food mixer and whisk well.

Add in the pouring cream and whisk for a moment or two until still quite loose in consistency.

Finally fold in the melted jelly and continue to whisk (by hand) for another twenty seconds or thereabout.

The mixture should still just be in the semi-whipped state at this time.

Pour the mixture in on top of the biscuit base.

Transfer to the fridge and allow to set properly, preferably overnight.

Remove the ring from around the side of the cheesecake, spread with the whipped cream and drizzle the remaining 4oz/110g lemon curd cover the top of the cheesecake in a haphazard fashion and scatter with the passion fruit seeds.

Edward's Top Tips:
Make sure the jelly has cooled before adding to the cream mixture.
As a 'get out of jail free' card, if your mixture gets too thick just whisk in another 4floz/110ml of pouring cream and continue as normal.
Digestive biscuits can be used instead of the gingernuts.

Rhubarb Pannacotta Serves 6

This is my own twist on stewed rhubarb and cream.
Feel free to vary the fruits. This dessert is quite rich so is best served at the end of a light meal.

Pannacotta:
2 leaves gelatine
12floz/350ml cream
3oz/75g sugar

Rhubarb Compote:
5-6 sticks rhubarb
3oz/75g caster sugar
2 tablespoons water
1 teaspoon grenadine syrup, optional

Begin by making the rhubarb compote.
Chop the rhubarb into chunks and place into a medium-sized saucepan with the sugar and water.
Cook on a medium heat for approximately 7-10 minutes, or until the rhubarb has softened.
Add the grenadine (if using) for additional colour at this stage.
Allow to cool.
Select six fancy glasses to serve the pannacotta. I think martini glasses or champagne flutes are nice. Glass yoghurt jars can also look very attractive.
Divide the rhubarb compote between the glasses or jars. Fill the chosen glass about a third of the way up and leave to rest.
Meanwhile soak the leaves of gelatine in cold water ensuring that they are fully immersed.
Place the cream and sugar into a large saucepan and bring slowly to the boil. Take the boiling cream mixture off the heat.
Strain the water off the gelatine using a sieve, not your hands. Give it a good shake to get rid of excess water and add it to the boiling cream.
Whisk the mixture continuously to make sure that the gelatine has broken down and is fully incorporated into the mixture. Allow it to cool down slightly and then divide it between the glasses.
Be careful when pouring in the cream mixture – try to keep it separate from the rhubarb compote.
Transfer to the fridge to set for 5-6 hours, or overnight.

Edward's Top Tips:
Feel free to substitute gooseberries, raspberries or any other type of fruit for the rhubarb.
Sometimes I just serve some pannacotta in a shot glass as a pre-dessert or as part of a dessert tasting plate.

A Cup of Crumble *Serves 6*

This, if I do say so myself, is a fantastic dessert! It looks very sophisticated yet quirky and tastes absolutely divine. It makes a great dinner-party dessert and you can have the entire dessert assembled in advance and then just bake it when it is required. Bear in mind that you can alter this recipe to use up other bits and pieces you have lying around.

Fruit Compote:
3 large cooking apples, peeled and diced
4oz/110g caster sugar
2 tablespoon water
5oz/150g fresh/frozen mixed berries

Crumble:
7oz/200g plain flour
3oz/75g brown sugar
4oz/110g butter
2oz/50g flaked almonds
½ teaspoon cinnamon

Place the apples, sugar and water in a medium-sized saucepan and bring to a gentle boil. Add in the berries and stir gently to incorporate them with the apples. Simmer on a low heat for 5-6 minutes until the fruit just starts to soften. Taste the fruit and add a little more sugar if you feel it is required. I normally like to leave it a little tart as the crumble topping is quite sweet.
Preheat the oven to 180C/350F/Gas Mark 4.
Meanwhile prepare the crumble topping by sieving the flour into a large bowl. Add in the brown sugar and the butter and rub the butter into the flour and sugar mixture with your fingertips until a fine consistency has been achieved.
Mix in the cinnamon and the flaked almonds at this stage and stir well.

Divide the fruit compote mixture between six oven-proof tea cups or small ramekins, filling them between half and two thirds of the way up and topping with some of the crumble topping.
(You may have some crumble topping left over that you can freeze for another time).
Place the cups onto a flat baking tray and put into the preheated oven and bake for approximately 20-25 minutes until the crumble topping is golden brown.
Place on a saucer and serve immediately with a little freshly-whipped cream.

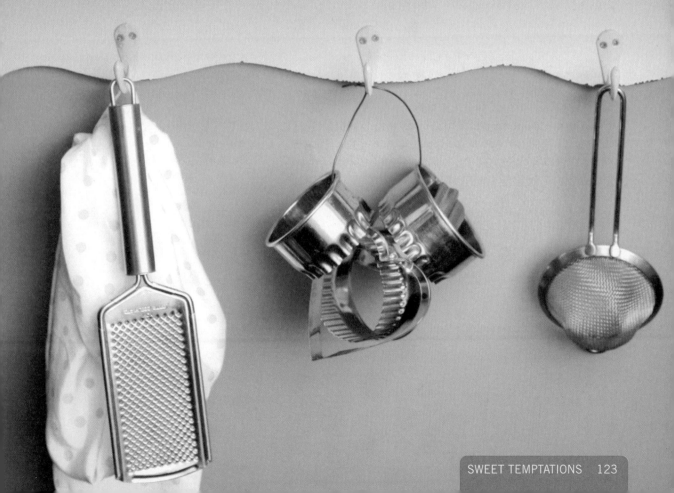

heavenly cakes & bakes

Mummy's Chocolate Buns *12 Buns*

People often ask me where my interest in cooking came from, and my answer is always the same: when we were growing up my mother baked every day – chocolate cake, queen of puddings, brown bread and much more. Nowadays, she bakes less, but this recipe is still her undefeated 'best hit' with all the family; even now as adults her children will still flock home for 'Mummy's chocolate buns'.

Buns:
4oz/110g butter, softened
4oz/110g caster sugar
8oz/225g plain flour
1 rounded teaspoon baking powder
3 large eggs

Filling:
3 tablespoons raspberry jam
5oz/150g milk chocolate
2 tablespoons coloured sugar strands

Preheat the oven to 180C/350F/Gas Mark 4.
Lightly grease a twelve-cup shallow bun tray. I choose not to use bun papers, but you can if you wish.
In a large mixing bowl cream the butter and sugar until they are light and fluffy. Add the three eggs to the mixture.
Sieve the baking powder and flour into the buttery mixture, then continue to cream the mixture together lightly until a smooth dropping consistency has been achieved.
(You may or may not need to add one or two tablespoons of milk at this stage if your mixture is a little dry. Mum has great belief in adding an extra egg yolk at this stage for added richness).
Divide the mixture between the twelve cups of the bun tin and pop the tray into the oven for approximately 18-20 minutes or until the buns are golden brown.
When they have cooled, split them across the middle (horizontally) and spread with a little layer of raspberry jam. Stick the bun back together again.
Meanwhile melt the milk chocolate in a heatproof bowl over a saucepan of simmering water and spread some melted chocolate on top of the buns. Scatter with some coloured sugar strands and allow to set.
Store in an airtight container until required.

Edward's Top Tip:
3oz/75g of sultanas or cherries can be added to the mixture for a fruity variation.
If desired you could pipe some flavoured butter cream on the top instead (p 137).

Never-Fail Muffins 12 Muffins

Muffins are such a popular item for children's lunch boxes or birthday parties. They are also a wonderful treat for long, lazy weekend breakfasts. This is a very basic recipe, and I've suggested a whole series of flavours that you can add to the mixture. Basically, you can have lots of fun playing around with different alternatives (and of course enjoying the fruits of your labour!)

1lb/450g plain flour
6ozs/175g caster sugar
1 rounded teaspoon of baking powder
4ozs/110g butter

2 large eggs
6floz/175ml milk
Flavouring of choice

Preheat oven to 180C/350F/Gas Mark 4.
Line a 12 cup muffin tray with muffin paper cases.
Mix flour, sugar and baking powder together.
Rub in the butter with the tips of your fingers.
Break in the eggs and milk and mix to a stiff batter.
Add in the flavouring of your choice at this stage and mix well.
Spoon into muffin cases in a prepared muffin tin and bake for 20-25 minutes until golden brown and puffed up.

Dust with icing sugar and serve!
Alternatively, you could mix 3 tablespoons of icing sugar with little boiled water until it reaches a running consistency and drizzle haphazardly over the top of the muffins.

Suggested Flavour:
White chocolate & raspberry

Lemon & blueberry (pictured)
Chocolate chip
Apple & cinnamon
Banana & milk chocolate
Cranberry & sultana

Suggested Amount:
3oz/75g white chocolate chips & 3oz/75g fresh/frozen raspberries
Grated zest of 1 lemon & 5oz/150g blueberries
5oz/150g mixed chocolate chips
2 eating apples, diced & ½ teaspoon ground cinnamon
2 ripe bananas, mashed & 3oz/75g milk chocolate chips
4oz/110g fresh cranberries & 2oz/50g sultanas

Edward's Top Tip:
Before baking the muffins why not sprinkle some crumble topping over the top (p 122) to add a different texture to the muffins.

Almond Cake *Serves 8-10*

This cake has quite a good shelf life so it is perfect to have made in advance.
It's delicious split and filled with buttercream icing.
Also, a slice of this is an ideal lunchbox filler.

6 eggs
6oz/175g caster sugar
5oz/150g unsalted butter

4oz/110g plain flour
7oz/200g ground almonds

Preheat the oven to 180C/350F/Gas Mark 4.

Lightly grease an 8inch/20cm deep cake tin and place a circular disc of parchment paper on the base of the tin to prevent the cake from sticking.

Whisk the eggs and caster sugar in a large bowl set over a pot of simmering water for about 8-10 minutes, until it reaches the ribbon stage (this means that the mixture will double in volume and become very pale in colour, but well volumised).

Meanwhile melt the butter in a small pot and allow to cool slightly.

Sieve the flour and ground almonds together.

Add the dry ingredients to the aerated egg mixture and fold them in carefully.

Gently fold in the melted and cooled butter.

Pour the mixture into the lightly-greased baking tin and bake for approximately 35-40 minutes.

As with all sponges, when cooked, it should be springy to the touch and a skewer inserted in the middle should come away clean.

If you wish you could add some grated lemon or orange zest to the eggs and caster sugar at the start for a flavoured version of the cake.

Edward's Sinful Chocolate Cake   *Serves 8-10*

This cake does take a little bit of time to make, but it's well worth the effort. It's a rich chocolate cake filled and topped with a dark chocolate ganache. It is a real special-occasion dessert and is a chocoholic's dream.

Chocolate Sponge:

5oz/150g butter
4oz/110g icing sugar
4 eggs, separated
1oz/25g cocoa powder

2oz/50g ground almonds
4oz/110g soft flour
Pinch of salt
4oz/110g caster sugar

Preheat the oven to 180C/350F/Gas Mark 4.
Grease and line an 8inch/20cm round, loose-bottomed cake tin.
Cream the butter and the icing sugar.
Separate the eggs, then add the egg yolks to the butter mixture.
Sieve all of the dry ingredients (flour, cocoa, ground almonds) together.

Add the dry ingredients to the buttery mixture and mix until thoroughly combined. At this stage the mixture will be very dry (much like pastry).
Whisk the egg whites with the caster sugar. Beat half the egg white mixture into the butter mixture to loosen it up and then fold in the remainder.
Transfer into a greased tin and bake at for 25-30 minutes.

Dark Chocolate Ganache:

8oz/225g dark chocolate
10floz/300ml pouring cream

Place the cream in a medium-sized pot and allow to come to the boil.
Chop or grate the chocolate into a bowl.

Pour the boiled cream on top of the chocolate and mix until the chocolate is completely melted.
Use as required to coat and fill the cake.

Filling: 4 tablespoons raspberry jam

To assemble the chocolate cake:
Split the sponge into three layers.
Place one layer of sponge on a thin cake board (the exact same size as the cake).
Spread half the raspberry jam on top of this first layer of sponge. Spread this with approximately a quarter of the chocolate ganache.
Place another layer of sponge on top and spread it with the remaining raspberry jam. Again use a quarter of the chocolate ganache to spread over this layer of the sponge.
Place the third and final layer of sponge on top and flatten it down with your hands to make it even.
Place the cake (still on the cake board) on a wire rack, pour the remaining dark chocolate ganache onto the cake and, using a palette knife, spread the ganache to

allow it to coat the cake completely.
Allow to set for a few moments and then transfer to a large serving platter.
If you wish you can serve the cake with some fresh raspberries.

Edward's Top Tip:
When coating the cake I normally place the wire rack on top of a large sheet of parchment paper as some of the chocolate ganache will run off. You can transfer any of these 'spillages' to the fridge and allow to set and then using your hands mould them into chocolate truffles which you can put sitting on the top of the cake as added decoration. You could coat the truffles in some chopped and toasted almonds if you wished.

Edward's Special Chocolate Biscuit Cake   Serves 12

Chocolate biscuit cake is one of the recipes that I often make at home. It has become a very popular choice for wedding cakes also. Chocolate biscuit cake tends to evoke memories of childhood; when we were growing up it was one of the things my eldest sister Anne would make. She has lost her recipe now, but mine is a very simple and delicious alternative.

1 tin condensed milk
4oz/110g butter
8oz/225g dark chocolate

1lb/450g selection of biscuits or bars
(Digestive, Rich Tea, Twix, Gingernuts, Mars Bars, Toffee-pops)

Lightly grease a 2lb/900g loaf tin.
Line the tin with a triple layer of cling film.
Gently heat the condensed milk, butter and chocolate together. Stir carefully as it has a tendency to burn.
Add the biscuits and bars – just throw them in and mash them up very roughly in the chocolate mixture.
Pour the mixture into the prepared loaf tin and leave in the fridge for 5-6 hours.
Cut with a sharp knife and serve.

Edward's Top Tip:
You could also try adding in these additional ingredients:
Sultanas/raisins
Cherries
Marshmallows
Chocolate Crunchie bars

Traditional Porter Cake *Makes 1 cake*

I love baking different styles of cakes. In our house fruit cake – of any variety – is very popular. This cake is versatile, quickly and easily made and, though it tastes good fresh from the oven, it is best kept for about a week in an airtight container. The cake is quite rich and it lasts very well for a couple of weeks (if it actually will last that long in your house). Sometimes I even use it as the base for a very rich and fruity bread and butter pudding or instead of the sponge part of a baked Alaska.

1lb/450g plain flour
Pinch of salt
1 rounded teaspoon baking powder
½ teaspoon cinnamon
½ teaspoon ground nutmeg
8oz/225g demerara sugar
8oz/225g butter
1lb/450g mixed dried fruit (sultanas, currants, raisins)

4oz/110g mixed peel
Grated zest of one orange
1 large tablespoon black treacle
12floz/350ml Guinness (porter)
2 eggs (beaten)
To Garnish:
2 tablespoons apricot jam

Preheat oven 180C/350F/Gas Mark 4.
Line a 8inch/20cm round cake tin with greaseproof paper. Make sure the tin is well greased so as to allow the cake to just slip out when it is cooked.
In a large bowl sieve the plain flour with the baking powder, cinnamon, nutmeg and salt. Mix these ingredients well to make sure the baking powder is well dispersed.
Add in the sugar and the butter. Rub the butter into the mix with your fingertips until it resembles breadcrumbs. At this stage add in the mixed dried fruit, mixed peel and orange zest and mix well.
In a separate bowl whisk together the eggs, treacle and Guinness and add into the dry ingredients. Beat well with a wooden spoon until well combined. Ensure that there is no trace of the dry ingredients at the bottom of the bowl. Pour the cake mixture into the previously-prepared tin and bake on the middle shelf of the preheated oven for

45 minutes. At this stage, reduce the heat to 150C/300F/Gas Mark 2 for a remaining hour and a quarter or until a skewer inserted in the cake comes out clean.
Allow the cake to cool in the tin and then remove the cake and place it on a serving platter.
Place the apricot jam in a small saucepan with a tablespoon of water and bring to a rapid boil.
Brush the cake with the boiled apricot jam, which will give a really nice glaze to the cake.
The cake is now ready to be served – and is delicious either hot or cold!

Edward's Top Tip:
Check the cake after an hour and if it is browning too quickly, cover with a double layer of greaseproof paper or tinfoil until baked.

Aunt Mary's Pink Cake   Serves 8-10

This is a very well-known cake in our family. My Aunt Mary was a wonderful cook and all family occasions were celebrated with her special 'pink cake'. As a very young child I would play cards (Newmarket was the game we played) with my aunts, Mary and Bridie, on a Sunday afternoon. Each week my Aunt Bridie provided the prizes for the card game – anything from stationery sets to cooking utensils. After the game, we three card sharks would end the session with a cup of tea and pink cake!

Sponge
8oz/225g softened butter
8oz/225g sugar
4 eggs
8oz/225g self-raising flour

Butter cream
4oz/110g softened butter
8oz/225g icing sugar
½ teaspoon pink food colouring
1 dessertspoon boiled water

Additional Requirements:
2 tablespoons raspberry jam

To make sponge:
Preheat oven to 180C/350F/Gas Mark 4.
Grease and line two 8inch/20 cm sandwich tins (round, square or heart shaped).
In a large mixing bowl cream the butter and sugar together until light and fluffy, add the eggs and flour and mix completely.
Pour into prepared cake tins and bake for 20-25 minutes or until the mixture comes away from the sides of the tin and a skewer inserted in the centre comes out clean.
Turn out onto a cooking rack and allow to cool completely.

To make butter icing:
Add the softened butter and icing sugar to a large bowl or electric mixer and beat until light and fluffy.
You should leave this to beat for approximately 8-10 minutes.
To soften the icing further I normally add the boiled water, to give a nice creamy consistency, and the pink food colouring.
Beat well ensuring that the colour is well incorporated.

Assembly:
Put one cake on the serving platter. Spread lightly with raspberry jam.
On the other cake arrange a layer of pink butter icing and stick this iced cake (icing side down) onto the jam coated layer.
Use the remaining icing to spread over the top of the cake.
Use a fork to create a criss cross pattern on the top.

potted pleasure

Cranberry & Orange Relish   Makes 1 x 1lb jar

You will never again return to the shop-bought cranberry sauce after tasting this delicious relish; it also makes a wonderful gift for friends.

10oz/300g fresh cranberries
3oz/75g caster sugar
Juice & zest of 1 orange

2floz/50ml water
1 cinnamon stick

Simply add all the ingredients to a pot and bring to the boil.

Gently simmer for 10-12 minutes until the majority of the liquids have reduced. By now, the sauce should have a nice crimson-red colour, and it should be thick and pulpy.

Transfer to a warm, sterile jar; this relish has a shelf life of approximately three months.

Edward's Top Tip:
You can stir a couple of spoons of this relish into gravies or festive stuffings for a deliciously fruity alternative. Sometimes I like to use two tablespoons of this relish to stir into some cooked apples and use it as an alternative option when making A Cup of Crumble (Page 122).

How to sterilise jars:
To sterilise the jars, wash them out with boiling water and then place them in a warm oven (130C/250F/Gas Mark ½) for approximately 15-20 minutes until completely dry. Wash the lids in boiling water and allow them to dry in a warm place.

Beetroot Relish   *Makes 2 x 1lb jars*

The colour of this beetroot pickle is most inviting and, like the rest of my relishes, it makes a very attractive gift to give to your friends. I normally serve this as part of a salad platter, and it is exceptionally good with baked ham.

½ tablespoon oil
14oz/400g whole beetroot, cooked and diced into cubes (see below)
1 medium-sized onion
3 large cooking apples

4oz/110g light brown sugar
¼ teaspoon ginger
3½ floz/100ml red wine vinegar
Pinch of salt

Dice the onion into rough chunks.

Peel, core and dice the cooking apples.

Heat a tiny amount of oil in a large pan and gently sweat the cooking apples with the onions for 4-5 minutes until they are softened.

Add the ground ginger and brown sugar and allow them to melt a little.

Add the prepared beetroot, together with the salt and the red wine vinegar, and allow to cook over a low heat for approximately forty minutes, until all the liquid has evaporated off.

Transfer the relish into warm sterile jars (see p140) and use as required.

As with most chutneys and preserves it is best to leave it to rest for a few weeks before using so as to allow the flavours to develop.

The chutney will last, unopened, for 4-6 months.

To cook the beetroot:

Bring a pan of unsalted water to the boil.

Drop in the beetroot (unpeeled) and allow the water to come back to the boil.

Simmer for approximately 45 minutes or until a knife inserted in the centre meets with little or no resistance, allow to cool, then peel and use as required.

Alternatively, you can by pre-cooked, whole beetroot in the supermarket.

Spiced Autumn Fruit Chutney

Makes approx 2 x 1lb jars

This is yet another delicious chutney that I like to have on standby for cold meat and cheese. It's also excellent as a topping for a homemade cheeseburger. Alternatively, use it to add a sharp cut to chicken liver paté.

8 ripe plum tomatoes, chopped roughly
2 large cooking apples, diced
1 green pepper, diced
2oz/50g sultanas
2oz/50g dried apricots, diced
1 large onion, chopped roughly

1 teaspoon of paprika/cayenne pepper
½ teaspoon of ground ginger
½ teaspoon of ground cloves
Pinch of salt
5oz/150g brown sugar
6floz/175ml white wine vinegar

Place all the ingredients in a large pot.
Bring the mixture slowly to the boil and then reduce to a very gentle simmer for an hour or until the tomatoes are soft and the liquid has partly evaporated off.
Transfer to warm sterile jars (p 140) and use as required.
This can be stored for up to a year.

Apple & Pear Chutney Makes 2 x 1 lb jars

This chutney is delicious served with a variety of cooked meats, but my favourite dish to serve it with is roasted pork. If this is nicely presented it looks fabulous given as a gift to someone as part of an edible gift hamper.

1 tablespoon oil
6 large firm pears, roughly diced
2 large cooking apples, roughly diced
1 medium onion, roughly chopped
3oz/75g dried apricots, chopped roughly

3oz/75g sultanas
½ teaspoon ground cloves
1 level teaspoon of ground ginger
5oz/150g light brown sugar
6floz/175ml cider vinegar

Heat the oil in a large saucepan.
Add the apples and pears, together with the onions, to the large saucepan and sauté for 5-6 minutes until just starting to soften at the edges.
Next add the sultanas, apricots, ground cloves and the ground ginger.
Stir these ingredients around in the pan for a few minutes until all of the fruit is coated with a film of spice.
Next, add in the brown sugar and the vinegar and bring this mixture to the boil – be careful, as it does have a tendency to burn!
Simmer for a further thirty minutes until part of the liquids are reduced and it has thickened.
Transfer to warm sterilised jars (p140) and seal.
Store until required.
The chutney will last for up to 6 months.

Red Onion Marmalade *Makes 1 medium jar*

4 medium red onions, peeled and thinly sliced.
3oz/75g dark brown sugar

3 tablespoons red wine
3 tablespoons red wine vinegar
1 teaspoon of oil

In a large pot, heat the onions and the oil over a high heat. Stir the contents constantly to move the onions around and prevent them from sticking.

As the onions begin to colour and soften (after about three minutes) add in the dark brown sugar and continue to stir. The sugar will begin to melt and will coat all of the onions.

Allow the sugar syrup to come to the boil gently.

Next, add in the red wine and the red wine vinegar.

Allow the mixture to come to the boil and then simmer for about fifteen minutes or until all the liquid has evaporated off.

Make sure that you stir it occasionally to prevent anything sticking to the base of the pot.

Transfer to clean, sterilised jars (p140) and store in the fridge (it will keep for up to four weeks.)

Semi-Dried Tomatoes *Makes 1 medium jar*

These tomatoes are a delicious alternative to the versions you can buy in the supermarket or delicatessen. I normally use plum tomatoes, but any kind of tomatoes are fine. Make sure they are nice and ripe though!

Bunch of mixed fresh herbs – parsley, basil, thyme, rosemary, sage, oregano (choose a selection)
6 plum tomatoes
Salt & freshly-ground black pepper

Pinch of sugar
1 tablespoon basil leaves, shredded
2 cloves garlic, thinly sliced
Approx 6 tablespoons of olive oil

Preheat oven to 180C/350F/Gas Mark 4.
In a small roasting tray spread out a layer of the herbs that you're using.
Quarter the tomatoes and place them on top of the herbs; season with salt, sugar and black pepper and place in the preheated oven for about an hour, until cooked. At this stage the tomatoes should still be nice and juicy, but should look partially dry and somewhat shrivelled.
Allow to cool and then place in a sterilised jar (p140).
Sprinkle with the shredded basil and slivers of the garlic.
Cover with olive oil and close the jar.
These tomatoes can be stored in your fridge for between one and two weeks, once they are kept covered in oil.

Edward's Top Tips:
Why not use the semi-dried tomatoes to make a delicious tomato pesto to top some fish prior to baking?
You could also use stir them into some cooked pasta or use them to garnish a salad.
You can use this method of semi drying for whole or halved cherry tomatoes also – just reduce the cooking time by about 15-20 minutes.
Basically, the herbs are used to raise the tomatoes so as not to leave them sitting in their own juices, which would hinder them from drying out. If it suited you better you could use a layer of rock salt or even use a grill tray with a wire rack included.

dining al fresco

Smoked Salmon & Goat's Cheese Ravioli   Serves 6-8

This, although it sounds like an unusual combination, is absolutely fantastic. It takes a little bit of effort and application, but it's well worth it.

Pasta:
9oz/250g pasta flour (available from good supermarkets)
1 teaspoon of salt
1 dessertspoon olive oil
2 eggs
3 egg yolks
Filling:
9oz/250g smoked salmon

5oz/150g goat's cheese
1 tablespoon of fresh parsley, chopped
Salt & pepper
Lemon Butter:
7oz/200g butter
Zest & juice of 1 lemon
1 tablespoon fresh parsley, chopped
Additional Requirements:
1 egg, lightly beaten

Begin by making the pasta dough:
Sift the flour and salt into a large mixing bowl or food processor.
Whisk the oil into the eggs and egg yolks and add to the flour.
Mix thoroughly by hand or in a food processor until the entire mixture has come together.
Knead gently for 5-10 minutes until a soft dough is achieved.
Cover with cling film and rest in the fridge for at least half an hour or until required.
After it's been allowed to rest in the fridge, pass the pasta mixture through a pasta machine, or roll out very thinly with a rolling pin, ensuring the pasta dough is very thin.
Using a biscuit cutter, cut out large rounds.
Next, dice the smoked salmon into very small dice and crumble the goat's cheese over it.
Add the chopped parsley and season lightly with salt and pepper.

Mash this salmon and cheese mixture up a little to ensure that everything is properly blended together.
Brush each circular piece of pasta dough lightly with the beaten egg.
Place a small amount of the filling in the centre and place another disc of pasta dough on top. Secure the edges with a fork dipped in flour, to prevent them from opening during the cooking process. It would be best at this stage to transfer the ravioli to the fridge to allow them to rest and firm up before cooking.
Meanwhile, to make the lemon butter, heat the butter in a small pot with the lemon zest and juice, then add the chopped parsley.
Bring a saucepan of water to the boil and add a little salt and olive oil.
Plunge the ravioli into the water and cook for 3-4 minutes or until they come to the surface.
Serve the ravioli in a warmed bowl and drizzle with the lemon butter and cracked black pepper.

Quiche Lorraine Serves 6-8

Quiche Lorraine is a very tasty tart and is so easy to make – perfect for a picnic or for dinner on the terrace. It is vitally important to take care when blind baking the pastry for this tart. It can be served either hot or cold, but I think it's best served with lingering warmth.

Shortcrust Pastry:
10oz/300g plain flour
Pinch of salt
5oz/150g butter
A couple of tablespoons of ice cold water

Filling:
6 thick rashers of bacon, diced
1 onion, diced
4 large eggs
2floz/50ml cream
½ pint/250ml milk
Fresh parsley, chopped
Salt & pepper
4oz/110g gruyère cheese

Sieve the flour into a large mixing bowl and add a pinch of salt.

Rub the butter into the flour and salt mixture until it resembles very fine breadcrumbs.

Mix in just enough ice cold water to bring the mixture together and then knead the pastry gently.

Cover with cling film and rest in the fridge for at least half an hour or until required.

Preheat the oven to 190C/375F/Gas Mark 5.

Roll out the pastry and use it to line a 9inch/23cm loose-bottomed flan dish with the pastry and blind bake in the oven (p 11).

Allow to cool.

To make the filling, fry the bacon and onion quickly in a large pan until cooked through and then spread them over the base of the pastry. Sprinkle on the cheese at this stage.

In a separate bowl, beat the eggs, milk and cream together with the seasoning and chopped parsley.

Pour this savoury egg custard onto the bacon and onion filling in the tartlet case.

Transfer to the preheated oven and bake for 25-30 minutes until the egg custard is set.

Serve with a large green salad.

Warm Salad of Baby Potatoes, Chorizo, Black Pudding & Rocket   Serves 6

The combination of flavours in this dish is really very good. I love the hint of spice which the chorizo gives – it works a treat with the fresh peppery rocket. Once you have all of the preparatory work done it is easy to build this salad and you can be as imaginative as you like with the presentation.

9 slices of black pudding (approximately 1 packet)
3oz/75g chorizo, diced
2 shallots, thinly sliced
9 baby potatoes
3 sprigs of fresh thyme
1 large bunch fresh rocket or lettuce leaves
A couple of spoons of mustard-seed dressing
Some sundried tomatoes, to garnish

Mustard-Seed Dressing: (stores in the fridge for approximately 2 weeks)
1 teaspoon of wholegrain mustard
1 tablespoon of honey
Juice of ½ lemon
Cracked black pepper
6floz/175ml olive oil
2 teaspoons of hot water (optional)
½ teaspoon chopped fresh thyme

To make the dressing, mix the mustard, honey, lemon juice and seasoning together. Whisk in the oil and mix well. The consistency should be thick and emulsified. If you would like a slightly thinner dressing, correct the consistency by whisking in the hot water.

Whisk in the chopped thyme and allow the dressing to rest until required.

Parboil the baby potatoes (put them into a pot with cold water, bring them to the boil and boil for approx 6-7 minutes until just tender) and allow to cool. Slice the potatoes into 4-5 slices each.

Heat a large frying pan and cook the black pudding on both sides, then add the baby potatoes, shallots and chorizo and cook them for a few minutes until browned. Sprinkle in the fresh thyme and season sparingly.

Meanwhile mix the rocket or lettuce leaves with a little of the dressing and place in the centre of your service plate/bowl. Just before you serve the dish divide the hot pudding mixture between the plates in a decorative fashion and garnish with some sundried tomatoes.

Edward's Top Tip:
If needs be (for entertaining purposes) you can cook the hot mixture a few minutes prior to the arrival of your guests. The cooked mixture can be kept warm in a relatively low oven for up to half an hour, which will make things easier on you, the host!

Slow-Cooked Sticky Pork Ribs   Serves 4-6

Pork ribs make a great family supper, and the beauty of this dish is that you can pop it into the oven and forget about it for a little while (being reminded only by the hungry family and the beautiful aroma from the oven)!

You'll need to allocate about 3 or 4 ribs per person. This is the perfect, finger-licking dish for eating outside on a summer evening.

3 cloves of garlic
2 tablespoons of thick honey
4floz/110ml dark soy sauce
7floz/200ml chicken stock
2 tablespoons of sweet chilli jam

2 pieces of star anise
Dash of Tabasco sauce
12-16 medium sized pork ribs (or 4 small racks of ribs)
½ tablespoon sesame seeds

Finely chop the garlic and put it in a large bowl with the honey, soy sauce, chicken stock, sweet chilli jam, Tabasco sauce and star anise. I normally break the star anise slightly so as to allow the full flavour to infuse.

Add the pork ribs to this marinade, mix well to ensure they are fully coated and leave to marinate for a couple of hours (or overnight to allow the ribs take on the full flavour and colour of the marinade).

Preheat the oven to 180C/350F/Gas Mark 4.

Transfer the ribs and marinade to a roasting tray, cover with tinfoil and cook for 1½-2 hours turning a couple of times throughout the process. After this time remove the tinfoil and cook for another half hour until the meat is tender, crispy and sticky.

Drizzle the remaining juices of the marinade over the sticky ribs, sprinkle with sesame seeds and serve with boiled basmati rice and salad.

Edward's Top Tip:
Use this marinade for pork chops, salmon pieces or chicken breast for fantastic, aromatic results.

Smoked Salmon Rolls *Serves 6-8*

This makes a delicious and quirky starter for a dinner party, but is also suitable for children's school lunchboxes or picnics. Although this recipe suggests pancakes, you could do something like this using tortilla wraps instead. They are also a fantastic canapé to serve with drinks.

Pancake batter: (makes 6 large pancakes)
8oz/225g plain flour
Pinch of salt
2 large eggs

1-2 dessertspoons fresh parsley, chopped
16floz/450ml milk
Grated zest of 1 lemon
½ tablespoon of oil or butter

In a large mixing bowl, sieve the flour and the salt together.
Break in the two large eggs and add the milk, whisking continuously until a smooth batter has been achieved. Add in the grated lemon zest and the chopped parsley at this stage also. Mix thoroughly until combined and then transfer into the fridge to rest for at least half an hour or until required.

Meanwhile heat a pan until quite hot. Add a little oil or butter to the pan and then spoon in some of the pancake batter and swirl quickly until the entire pan has been covered with the batter.
Allow to cook for a moment or two on either side until they are nice and golden brown.
Store the pancakes between discs of parchment paper and, if necessary, refrigerate until required.

Filling:
3 tablespoons crème fraiche
1 tablespoon parsley, chopped

Juice of 1 lemon
Cracked black pepper
Approx 12 slices of smoked salmon

Mix the crème fraiche, parsley, lemon juice and cracked black pepper together and store in a bowl.
Thinly slice the smoked salmon (or buy presliced).
Lay the pancakes out flat on a chopping board. Spread with some of the lemon-scented crème fraiche and then arrange some smoked salmon on top. Roll up very tightly and cut with a sharp knife into rounds, discarding the end slices. The rounds should be approximately an inch wide.
Arrange onto a large serving platter.
Serve immediately or transfer to the fridge.

Baked Mediterranean Chicken with Cheesy Spaghetti Serves 6

This is a great way of adding some robust flavours to chicken as the chorizo imparts a delicious smoky flavour.

6 small breasts of chicken

Stuffing:

4oz/110g chorizo (not pre-sliced), diced

3-4 tablespoons cream

6 sundried tomatoes

3oz/75g mozzarella cheese, grated

6 basil leaves

Place the chorizo and cream into a food processor and blitz until a coarse mousse-like consistency has been achieved.

Split the chicken breasts like a book and pop a spoon of the chorizo mixture, topped with a basil leaf, a sun dried tomato and some mozzarella cheese into each. Close the chicken breast tightly to secure the filling.

Preheat the oven to 180C/350F/Gas Mark 4.

Breadcrumb coating: (all measurements approximate in this section)

6oz/175g fresh white breadcrumbs

1 tablespoon sesame seeds

1oz/25g plain flour

1 egg mixed with 3 ½ floz/100ml milk

Fill three bowls:

Bowl 1: Plain flour with the addition of salt and pepper

Bowl 2: 1 egg mixed with milk

Bowl 3: Breadcrumbs mixed with sesame seeds

Pass the chicken through the three bowls. Firstly coat the chicken in the seasoned flour, shake off the excess flour and pass into the egg wash mixture and lastly coat generously in the sesame and breadcrumb mixture. Pat the crumb to the chicken breast with your hand.

Heat a frying pan with a little oil and cook the crusted chicken on both sides for approximately three minutes. Transfer the crusted chicken breasts to the preheated oven for a further 20-25 minutes just to ensure the chicken is well cooked through.

Cheesy Spaghetti:

12oz/350g fresh or dried spaghetti

5floz/150ml pouring cream

3floz/75ml/½ glass white wine

3oz/75g freshly grated mozzarella

Cook the spaghetti according to the packet instructions. Drain the spaghetti.

Put all of the above ingredients for the sauce into a pot and bring to the boil for five minutes and then mix in with the cooked spaghetti and serve with the baked Mediterranean chicken.

Mediterranean Vegetable Stack *Serves 6-8*

This is a fantastic vegetarian recipe, and perfect for eating outdoors!

4-5 tortilla wraps
8oz/225g mozzarella cheese, grated
Filling:
1 aubergine
1 courgette
1 red onion

1 each of red, green, yellow pepper
2x14oz/400g tin of tomatoes (fresh plum tomatoes could also be used)
6-8 mushrooms, sliced
4 cloves of garlic, crushed
½ teaspoon dried mixed herbs

Slice all of the vegetables into evenly-shaped pieces. Gently heat a large saucepan, then add oil to the pot and fry the vegetables and crushed garlic until they are all glazed and beginning to soften.
Pour in the chopped tomatoes (or fresh if you prefer) and mixed herbs at this stage and allow the mixture to cook very gently on a nice low heat for about forty-five minutes. Season accordingly and serve or store, as required.

Assembly:
(This can be made up in advance)
Lay a tortilla wrap on the base of a flat baking tray.
Fill with the vegetable mixture (and some of the grated mozzarella) and repeat this process.
Repeat until you have four or five layers.
Finish with a tortilla wrap on the top, sprinkled with some of the grated cheese.
Heat the oven to 190C/375F/Gas Mark 5 and bake the stack for 15-20 minutes until bubbling hot. Serve with a large green salad.

Curried Barbequed Chicken Breasts Serves 6-8

This is a nice, fiery option and is definitely not for the faint-hearted. I think the marinade works really well as the robust flavour suits chicken. This chicken, when cooked, is also lovely to put into a pitta bread with some shredded lettuce and cucumber.

4-6 chicken breasts
3½floz/100ml natural yoghurt
2 rounded teaspoons green curry paste
Juice of ½ lime

1 dessertspoon oil
1 dessertspoon parsley or coriander, freshly-chopped
Cracked black pepper

Begin by splitting the chicken breasts in two so as to make them easier to cook through on the barbecue. It is best to slice them in half lengthways, so that you're left with two thin fillets instead of one thicker one. Alternatively, you could just cover the full chicken breast with a freezer bag or cling film and use a rolling pin to flatten it and make it thinner.

To make the marinade:
Put the curry paste into a large mixing bowl and add in the lime juice and the oil and whisk thoroughly. Mix in the yoghurt, chopped coriander and cracked black pepper and again mix well.

(If you want a very robust green colour for the curry marinade, you could put all of the ingredients into a food processor and blitz thoroughly.)

Place the chicken breasts into the marinade and allow to marinate for a couple of hours (or overnight if time allows) to infuse a wonderful curried flavour into the chicken.

Heat the barbecue or chargrill pan and cook the thin chicken breasts for about 4-5 minutes on either side. Putting the lid on the barbecue creates a sort of oven effect. Don't turn the chicken too early as it will stick to the bars of the grill.

Edward's Top Tips:
On a cold winter's night, why not consider marinating some whole breasts of chicken and roasting them in the oven?
You can also use the marinade on diced chicken pieces, which you could use for a delicious stir fry or curry.

Honey & Ginger Vegetable Skewers on the Barbeque _Serves 6_

A fantastic vegetarian option for the barbeque!

You can use whatever selection of vegetables you wish, just try to bring as much colour as possible to the dish!

Skewers:

1 red pepper

1 courgette

1 aubergine

6 mushrooms

6 cherry tomatoes

1 red onion, cut into wedges

For the marinade:

2 cloves of garlic, crushed and chopped

1 inch/2cm root ginger, chopped finely

Juice and zest of one orange

2 tablespoons honey

1 tablespoon oil

½ teaspoon dried chilli flakes

Salt & freshly-ground black pepper

Prepare marinade by simply whisking all the ingredients together.

Then dice the courgette, aubergine and red pepper into bite-size cubes.

Thread onto six metal skewers with the cherry tomatoes, mushrooms and red onion wedges and arrange on a flat baking tray.

Pour the marinade over them, and allow to rest for up to two hours.

Preheat the barbecue and cook the skewers for 3-4 minutes on each side, using the additional marinade to baste the vegetables during cooking.

Serve with some baked potatoes and green salad.

drinks to go

Homemade lemonade

When we were young children we would often go out for a 'Sunday drive'; this would be enlivened by a big basket of sandwiches, chocolate buns (p 127) and bottles of delicious homemade lemonade. When pondering philosophically about life situations, I am often reminded of the old cliché, 'When life gives you lemons just make lemonade'. In other words turn something sour into something good, and this lemonade is definitely something good!

4 large lemons
4oz/110g caster sugar
1 pint/600ml water

Garnish:
Soda or sparkling water
Lemon wedges
Mint sprigs
Ice cubes

Thinly slice the lemons and place in a wide-based saucepan, along with the sugar and the water.
Bring to the boil and simmer for 6-7 minutes.
Turn off the heat and, using a wooden spoon, press and squash the lemon slices to ensure that the juice is going into the water.
When the lemon mixture has cooled a little, set a large sieve over a glass jug, strain the mixture into the jug and transfer to the fridge to allow to cool completely.
When the mixture is cool, taste it to ensure you are happy with the flavour, adding a little extra sugar if required. Although this mixture can be served as it is, I prefer to half-fill a large jug of ice with the lemon mixture and top up with some soda or sparkling water. Add in some mint sprigs and lemon wedges and serve immediately to thirsty family and friends!

Sangria

'Me gusta traer un vaso de sangria!'

A number of years ago when I took a conversational Spanish class, I had to learn lots of different phrases for use when holidaying in Spain. The above phrase was the opening line you'd use when ordering a drink in a Spanish bar; it means, 'I would like to order a glass of Sangria.'

Years later, I'm not sure how many of my Spanish phrases I have needed, but funnily enough this one has often been called upon!

3 tablespoons brandy
1 tablespoon honey
3floz/100ml freshly-squeezed orange juice
1 bottle of red wine (Spanish Rioja works wonderfully)

1 orange, sliced
1 eating apple, cut into wedges
5-6 strawberries, sliced
1 mango, cut into wedges

Mix the brandy and honey together in a large measuring jug and then add in the freshly-squeezed orange juice.
Place the sliced fruit in a large serving jug, then pour in the honey, brandy and orange mixture.
Top the jug up with red wine and mix well.
Leave to rest for up to an hour to allow all the flavours to blend together.

Edward's Top Tip:
I like to serve my sangria chilled, so I would either store it in the fridge or serve it with some crushed ice, but some of the purists amongst you might prefer to serve it at room temperature.
And remember 'Much wants more'!
Olé!

Lemon & Raspberry Bellini

Travel and glamorous TV shows have made us all *au fait* with flamboyant drinks over the last number of years. Normally, when we hear of the famous Italian Bellini, it's peach flavour, but here I've chosen to opt for a lemon & raspberry alternative.

1 bottle of good quality Prosecco
Lemon & Raspberry Purée:
2 lemons, thinly sliced

8oz/225g fresh or frozen raspberries
3½ floz/100ml cold water
3oz/75g caster sugar

Place the raspberries, lemon slices, water and sugar into a medium-sized saucepan and bring to the boil.
Simmer for 4-5 minutes and then turn off the heat.
Once the mixture has cooled a little, strain it into a jug through a fine sieve, making sure to squeeze all the goodness from the lemons and raspberries.

Transfer the purée into a small bottle and store in the fridge until required.
Select six large champagne flutes and fill them up a third of the way with the raspberry purée.
Top up the glass with the Prosecco and replenish as much as you like!

The Perfect Irish Coffee

So many people treat themselves to an Irish coffee on occasion and when made correctly they are a fantastic way to end a meal. I love to serve them at the end of a dinner party. You need to take your time preparing it and you will lose marks from your guests if the cream sinks to the bottom. If the cream does sink it will still be delicious. Practice makes perfect. Think of all the fun you can have practising!!

2 cups of strong, hot, black coffee
4 teaspoons brown sugar

2 tablespoons Irish whiskey
3 tablespoons thick cream

Warm two large glasses, put a teaspoon down in each and fill them up two thirds of the way with the strong, black coffee.
Stir two teaspoons brown sugar into each.
Add a tablespoon of Irish whiskey to each and stir well.
Lightly whisk the cream until it is semi-whipped.
Remove the spoon and pour half the lightly-whipped cream over the back of the hot spoon into the glass, allowing the cream to slide in slowly. Pour the cream slowly as rushing, at this critical stage, will cause the cream to sink. Repeat with the other coffee and serve immediately.

Top Tips:
There are many variations to this recipe; you can have fun experimenting with at home by substituting different alcohol instead of the Irish whiskey.
French Coffee: Brandy
Calypso Coffee: Tia Maria
Bailey's Coffee: Bailey's Irish Cream

festive foods

Dad's Christmas Breakfast   Serves 6

My brother, sisters and I have so many memories of our absolutely fantastic childhood. Our house was quite traditional – my mother did most of the cooking – but on Christmas day my father always cooked breakfast for the family. In later years as our family numbers increased (in-laws!), I gave him a hand, but it was always his 'gig'. Every Christmas morning we were awoken (very early as I recall) by my father who would be 'taking breakfast orders' from each of us. Breakfast was always delicious and we laughed our way through it each year. The key to the dish is preparation. There are so many elements to it that sometimes it can seem as challenging as a three-course meal, but when executed correctly it's superb. The most important thing is to ensure everything is ready at the same time and piping hot.

6 tomatoes, halved
A little olive oil, for frying
Salt & freshly-ground black pepper
6 slices coarse white pudding
6 slices coarse black pudding
6 tomatoes, halved

8oz/225g mushrooms, sliced
1oz/25g butter
12 back bacon rashers, smoked or unsmoked
12 good quality butcher's sausages
6 eggs, to scramble, poach or fry (see opposite)
A little flat-leaf parsley, to garnish

Preheat the oven to 190C/375F/Gas Mark 5. Place the tomatoes on a small baking tray. Season the tomatoes lightly with a little salt and pepper, drizzle with a tiny amount of olive oil and bake in the oven for fifteen minutes until softened.

At this stage reduce the oven temperature to 140C/275F/Gas Mark 1, which will be a suitable temperature for storing food as it is cooked before service.

Heat a large frying pan or sauté pan with the butter and cook the mushrooms for approximately 5-6 minutes until cooked through. Season lightly with a little salt and pepper and keep warm until required.

Heat the frying pan with a tiny amount of oil and cook the black and white pudding on each side for 3-4 minutes until they are nice and crispy. Store in the oven until required.

Cook the sausages on the same pan until they are browned all over and cooked through to the middle. Again they can be stored in the oven until required.

Preheat the grill. Place the rashers under the grill and grill for approximately 4-5 minutes until golden brown. Cook the eggs of your choice (see opposite page).

Arrange all the food on a serving plate or on a large platter, garnish with a sprig of flat-leaf parsley and serve immediately.

Eggs:

Fried Eggs (you will need eggs and a little oil for frying):

Heat a small frying pan with some vegetable or sunflower oil.

Crack the egg into the pan and cook on a medium heat until the white sets sufficiently. Tilt the pan to one side and spoon the hot fat on top of the egg yolk until it firms up a little.

Serve immediately with a twist of cracked black pepper on the top.

Poached Eggs (you will need eggs and 1 teaspoon white wine vinegar):

Bring a medium-sized saucepan of water to the boil.

Drop in a teaspoon white wine vinegar and remove the saucepan from the heat.

Gently swirl the saucepan to move the water.

Carefully break in the eggs (no more than three at a time) into the saucepan and leave to set.

Cook for approximately 3-4 minutes until the egg yolks are just firm to the touch.

Drain with a slotted spoon and serve immediately.

Scrambled Eggs (you will need eggs and a little butter, a little cream and salt & pepper):

In a mixing bowl beat together three eggs and three tablespoons of cream with a little salt and pepper. Whisk well until combined.

Place a shallow-based saucepan on a medium heat. Place a teaspoon of butter onto the pan and then pour in the beaten egg mixture.

Stir continuously with a wooden spoon until the eggs have a fluffy consistency.

Serve immediately.

Edward's Buttered Turkey Serves 8-10

You just can't beat the traditional Christmas turkey!

16lb/7.25kg turkey
6 smoked rashers of bacon

Stuffing:

1 medium-sized onion, diced
4oz/110g butter
3oz/75g fresh cranberries
4 tablespoons of mixed herbs –parsley, sage, thyme etc – chopped

1 cooking apple, grated or finely chopped
12oz/350g fresh, white breadcrumbs
12oz/350g sausage meat
Salt & freshly-ground black pepper

Additional Ingredients:

3oz/75g butter, softened
1 tablespoon of mixed herbs – parsley, sage, thyme – chopped

Heat the butter in a medium-sized saucepan and gently fry the diced onion for 4-5 minutes until it has softened, but not yet coloured. At this stage add the cranberries and the chopped, mixed herbs and immediately turn off the heat. Allow this mixture to cool.

Put this 'buttery onion' mixture in a large mixing bowl, then add the grated apple, breadcrumbs and sausage meat. Season with salt and pepper.

Preheat the oven to 200C/400F/Gas Mark 6.

Using some cold, damp kitchen paper, wipe out the cavity of the turkey. I normally line the cavity with baking parchment, which makes the stuffing easy to remove when the turkey is cooked; once you have lined the cavity, pack the stuffing loosely into the bird.

Weight the turkey again, once it has been stuffed, to get a true measure of the cooking time.

Put the turkey onto a large roasting tray.

Mix the remaining butter and the remaining mixed herbs together.

Gently manoeuvre your hand under the skin of the turkey, just at the breast bone section, and spread the flesh with the softened herb butter, trying to get it spread evenly over the breasts. Lay the streaky rashers of bacon across the top of the buttered breasts to protect the meat and prevent it from drying out.

Loosely cover the turkey with some tinfoil, which you'll remove after the first two hours.

Put the turkey into the oven and begin to roast.

After the first hour reduce the temperature to 170C/325F/Gas Mark 3.

Cooking Times: Allocate twenty minutes per pound and then an additional 20-30 minutes in the oven. In total this turkey should take about 5½ hours. When a skewer is inserted into the meat nearest the bone (i.e. the leg) the juices should run completely clear and the leg, when pulled, should feel loose and ready to fall away.

Allow the meat to rest for at least half an hour after it comes out of the oven, then carve as required.

Edward's Top Tip:

There are different opinions when it comes to stuffing – should it be cooked in or out of the turkey – but I think it's fine to stuff the actual bird itself. However, I would remind you that if you are stuffing the turkey in advance you need to ensure that both the turkey and the stuffing are completely cold before you stuff the bird, because if you put hot or warm stuffing into the turkey and then leave it for a while the heat of the stuffing will begin to 'cook' the turkey slightly and can cause bacteria to form, which will increase the risk of food poisoning.

Christmas Pudding   *Serves 6-8*

This is a very simple Christmas pudding recipe and will be even more delicious if, once it's cooked, you continue to top it up with lots of whiskey or brandy for the few weeks before Christmas.

Fruit:
4oz/110g sultanas
4oz/110g raisins
4oz/110g currants
4oz/110g mixed peel, chopped
4oz/110g cherries, chopped

Dry Ingredients:
2oz/50g white breadcrumbs
4oz/110g dark brown sugar
3oz/75g plain flour

2oz/50g almonds, chopped
½ teaspoon mixed spice
½ teaspoon nutmeg, grated
½ teaspoon ground cinnamon

Wet Ingredients:
2 eggs
3oz/75g butter, melted
1 large cooking apple, stewed
4floz/110ml stout
1 measure whiskey, rum or brandy

Grease a 2lb/900g pudding bowl.

Then put all the fruit into a large mixing bowl along with all of the dry ingredients.

In a separate bowl combine the wet ingredients.

Next, combine the wet ingredients with the dry and fruit ingredients and mix thoroughly.

Place in the well-greased pudding bowl, cover with a disc of parchment paper and then a tightly-fitting lid.

Place the pudding bowl into a large saucepan half filled with water.

Bring the water to the boil and then reduce to a very gentle simmer.

Steam for six hours, making sure that the water does not boil off.

After the cooking time has elapsed remove the bowl from the water, take off the lid and greaseproof paper and allow the pudding to cool down completely.

When cold, re-cover as before with fresh paper and store till needed.

Serve with brandy butter.

Edward's Top Tips:
It's best to have the puddings steamed at least 4-6 weeks before Christmas to allow the fruit and the pudding to mature.

On Christmas Day, reheat the pudding (in portions) gently in the microwave or return to a pot of water for an hour to warm the entire pudding through to the centre.

If you have the time, you could soak the fruit in the stout or Irish whiskey for a day or two before making the pudding.

Vegetarian suet (which comes in a box, grated) can be used instead of melted butter.

Honey & Wholegrain Mustard-Glazed Loin of Bacon (St Patrick's Day) Serves 6-8

One of the most popular 'traditional Irish dishes' is bacon and cabbage, which on St Patrick's day features on both restaurant and household menus up and down the country. I have, in this particular version, given the traditional bacon a delicious crust that will be very well received by all your family and friends.

1 loin of bacon (approx 4lb6oz/2kg)
1 tablespoon wholegrain mustard
2oz/50g brown sugar

6 dessertspoons of honey
2floz/50ml water

Place the bacon in a large saucepan and cover with cold water. Bring to the boil, then reduce the heat and simmer for 1½ hours until completely tender.
Preheat the oven to 180C/350F/Gas 4.
Remove the bacon from the water and allow to cool for about twenty minutes.
Transfer the meat to a baking dish or roasting tray.
With a sharp knife make some incisions in the fat of the bacon in a criss-cross pattern; this will give a nice professional finish to the bacon.
Heat the water, honey, mustard and brown sugar in a small saucepan and allow them to come gently to the boil. When it's boiling, pour this mixture over the loin of bacon and transfer to the oven for 15-20 minutes, or until the bacon has achieved a nice, crunchy crust. The bacon has already been cooked, at this stage you are just allowing it to achieve a nice glaze.
Allow to cool slightly before serving.

Edward's Top Tip:
If you wish you could stud the bacon with some cloves as well for added flavour.

American-Style Pancakes (Shrove Tuesday)

Pancakes come in many styles – thick, thin, flavoured, plain; this recipe is for American-style pancakes, which rise very well. Pancakes, in some form, are eaten and enjoyed worldwide. In Ireland, pancakes are traditionally eaten on Shrove Tuesday, the eve of the beginning of Lent; Lent is a time of fast and abstinence, so in the past, pancakes were a great way of using up rich ingredients like eggs and butter in preparation. Nowadays pancakes are much more common and can be served either sweet or savoury.

Pancake Batter:
10oz/300g plain flour
2 large eggs
½ teaspoon baking powder
2oz/50g caster sugar
10floz/300ml buttermilk

Garnish:
Maple syrup
Cream, freshly-whipped
Fresh mixed berries

Sieve the plain flour and baking powder into a large bowl. Add in the sugar and mix well.

Break in the two eggs and mix a little. The mixture will be quite lumpy at this stage, but DON'T PANIC!

Mix in the buttermilk, little by little. Whisk well ensuring that you remove all lumps.

The batter should be a very thick, coating consistency.

Transfer to the fridge and allow to rest for up to an hour.

Heat some butter in a large frying pan, then drop three large tablespoons of batter onto the pan and allow to cook gently for 3-4 minutes before turning the pancake over onto the other side until it too is golden brown.

Transfer to a large serving platter and serve with some freshly-whipped cream, fruit and a side portion of maple syrup.

Enjoy. (And of course repeat this process for all other guest/family members!!)

Edward's Top Tip:
Pancakes can be stored on a plate in the oven to keep them warm whilst you are cooking a batch, although normally if you get the job of making the pancakes you are left standing at the pan, repeatedly cooking pancakes, as your family and friends scoff them.

Easter Simnel Cake Serves 10-12

Simnel Cake is a light fruit cake with a layer of almond paste (marzipan) baked in the centre of the cake for added moisture. Traditionally, the top of the cake is decorated with eleven balls of marzipan arranged around the exterior of the cake to represent the eleven true disciples of Jesus (Judas is omitted). Sometimes there may be a twelfth ball of marzipan placed in the centre of the cake to represent Jesus. It is a quintessential English and Irish tradition.

Fruit Cake:
2oz/50g ground almonds
1½ teaspoons mixed spice
¼ teaspoon ground nutmeg
6oz/175g self-raising flour
6oz/175g brown sugar
6oz/175g butter, softened
12oz/350g mixed fruit (sultanas, currants, mixed peel, cherries)
3 large eggs

Almond Paste:
4oz/110g icing sugar
8oz/225g ground almonds
4oz/110g caster sugar
2 large eggs
½ teaspoon almond essence
Juice of ½ lemon

Decoration:
A little apricot jam
Mini eggs or chicks, as decorations (optional)

To Make Almond Paste:
Sieve the ground almonds and icing sugar together.
Add the caster sugar and mix well.
In a separate bowl, whisk the eggs, lemon juice and almond essence with a fork and, then add two thirds of this liquid to the dry ingredients and bind them together. Do not add all of the liquid at once as you may or may not need it all depending upon the size of your eggs. Add the remaining liquid only if it is needed to bind the mixture together. The almond paste should look like a ball of pastry after it has been kneaded together.
Divide the paste into three, wrap each in cling film and store in the fridge until required.
(If you have made the almond paste the day before it is best to take it out of the fridge approximately half an hour before you need it as it does have a tendency to become quite firm in the fridge and rolling it out can be difficult.)

To Make the Cake:
Line an eight inch deep cake tin with baking parchment.
Sieve the ground almonds, self-raising flour, mixed spice and nutmeg together.
In a separate bowl, cream the butter and brown sugar together until light and fluffy.
Add in the eggs and sieved dry ingredients to the creamed butter and sugar and mix until thoroughly combined.
Carefully mix in the dried fruits and stir well to ensure that the fruit has become fully incorporated into the cake mix.

Assembly:

Preheat the oven to 150C/300F/Gas Mark 2.

Put half of the cake mixture into the tin and spread out so that it is nice and flat.

Roll out a third of the almond paste into an 8 inch disc and place it on top of the cake mix.

Pour the remaining cake mix on top of the almond paste and spread it out evenly.

Bake the cake for between 1½ hours-2 hours depending on the oven.

(A skewer inserted in the centre should come out clean.)

Check the cake after about an hour; if it's browning too much, loosely cover it with tinfoil.

Remove from the oven when cooked and allow the cake to cool completely.

Decoration:

Once the cake is cooled, brush the top surface of the cake with boiled apricot jam.

Roll out another third of the almond paste into a disc and arrange this on top of the cake.

Divide the remaining almond paste into eleven pieces, roll them into balls and secure around the top of the cake with a little apricot jam.

Brush the entire surface of the cake (i.e. the exposed almond paste) with beaten egg and return to a hot oven (190C/325F/Gas Mark 5) oven for 4-5 minutes or glaze with a chef's blow torch.

Garnish the cake with some mini eggs or Easter chicks if desired.

Colcannon (Halloween)

Colcannon is a familiar dish in Ireland; traditionally, it's served on Halloween. To this day, my mum often makes a big bowl of colcannon on a cold night; it's really delicious with homemade sausages.

6-7 large potatoes
1oz/25g butter
8oz/225g green curly kale (or other type of cabbage), shredded

2floz/50ml milk, warmed
1 bunch spring onions
Pinch fresh grated nutmeg (optional)
Salt & freshly-ground black pepper

Peel the potatoes, place in a medium-sized saucepan and cover with water.

Bring to the boil and allow to simmer until they are tender.

Remove from the heat, strain off the water and cover with a tightly-fitting lid for ten minutes to allow them to dry out/steam.

Mash the potatoes with the butter and a pinch of salt and pepper.

Plunge the shredded cabbage into boiling water and boil for 6-8 minutes until just tender, then strain and run under cold water until cool (this will stop the cooking process).

Pour the milk into a small saucepan and add the chopped spring onions and the cooked cabbage.

Allow this mixture to come to the boil, then add to the mashed potatoes, season with salt and pepper and heat until the entire mixture is piping hot.

Season with a little grated nutmeg if, desired.

Serve immediately.

menu suggestions

Menu Suggestions

Sometimes it can be hard to know what to serve when you're entertaining. But the trick is really to decide what sort of event you are cooking for – is it casual or formal, for example? You'll also need to consider how much time you'll have to prepare – are you rushing home from work to cook, or do you have all day to prepare something really special? To help you plan your menu, I've chosen a few recipes from this book to suit different occasions.

For a very classy dinner party, why not try:

Left: **Chilli Crab Salad with Smoked Salmon**
Something Fishy p 67

Above: **Fillet of Beef & Spring Onion Potato Cakes with Roast Shallot & Balsamic Reduction**
Mouthwatering Meat Dishes p 49

Left: **Rhubarb Pannacotta**
Sweet Temptations p 121

For a Family Sunday Lunch, why not try:

Right: **Baked Flat-Cap Mushrooms with Pine Nut Stuffing & Buffalo Mozzarella** Light Bites p 15

Above: **Slow Cider-Roasted Loin of Pork** Mouthwatering Meat Dishes p 57

Right: **Lemon, Ginger & Passion Fruit Cheesecake** Sweet Temptations p 118

If you are entertaining informally when time is scarce, why not try:

Left: **Pea & Broccoli Soup**
Super Soups p 30
Below: **Spicy Beef Fajitas with Cajun Potato Wedges**
Mouth-watering Meat Dishes p 54
Opposite: **A Cup Of Crumble**
Sweet Temptations p 122